THE AMERICAN WILD TURKEY

Books by John McDaniel

The Turkey Hunter's Book
Spring Turkey Hunting
The American Wild Turkey

THE AMERICAN WILD TURKEY

Reflections on the Bird, the Hunt, and the Hunter

JOHN McDANIEL

THE LYONS PRESS

DEDICATION

Jerry Rodgers—Turkey Hunter

Jerry Wilson Rodgers was born in Augusta County, Virginia on January 9, 1950. He died in the contiguous county of Rockbridge on February 22, 2000. Jerry was a member of that select group of great turkey hunters who chase the birds with passion, competence and integrity in those precious parts of America that are still wild.

Jerry was not born to wealth or high social status. He was not known outside our ridges and hollows; however, this book will argue that it is Jerry, and his like, who have been *the most important* custodians of, and contributors to, that remarkably successful cultural and political adventure known as The American Story.

Printed in the United States of America

10 9 8 7 6 5 4 3 2 1

Library of Congress Cataloging-in-Publication Data

McDaniel, John M.
   The American wild turkey : hunting tactics and techniques /
   John McDaniel.
      p. cm.
   ISBN 1-58574-037-3 (hc.)
      1. Turkey hunting. 2. Turkey hunting—Anecdotes.
      3. McDaniel, John M. I. Title.
   SK325.T8 M26 2000
   799.2'4645—dc21   00-020389

CONTENTS

INTRODUCTION

I wrote my first piece on turkey hunting in 1974. Ever since, I have regularly escaped the demands of college teaching to write. The chapters in this book were completed between 1974 and 1999. Nine were originally published, in different form, in one of my two previous works, *The Turkey Hunter's Book* (1980) and *Spring Turkey Hunting* (1986). Another was published in a local newspaper. The other thirty-one were written specifically for this book.

I am grateful to Jim Rickhoff, the editor of the Amwell Press, who published my first book, *The Turkey Hunter's Book*. It is ironic that I was introduced to Rickhoff by one of the characters I celebrate in this book, the late George Schielke. George was a gunsmith who had a shop near my childhood home. When I was a kid, my indulgent mother drove me to George's shop at least once a week. When Nell and I were married, George and his wife, Barbara, became our good friends and were important sources of advice, support, and encouragement. He was the first person, outside my family, who encouraged me to write.

The inspiration for this book can be traced to comments I received from readers of my first two books. While my primary goal in those books was to provide information about turkey-hunting skills, many people said they particularly enjoyed the anecdotes in both books. This is a collection of stories and essays about wild-turkey hunting. There are no specific data on how to hunt. I write to capture the essence of turkey hunting, celebrate the special characters who are great turkey hunters, and make a case for the American wild turkey. If I don't help you feel the thrills generated by turkey hunting, I will have failed. If the immense challenge of acquiring the skills necessary to becoming a competent turkey hunter is not obvious, I will have failed. If you do not learn why turkey hunting is so important to turkey hunters, I will have failed. If your respect for the wild turkey is not increased, I will have failed.

The book has been fun to write. I found myself working on it whenever I had a chance. I am convinced the stories are important. There are many tributes to the tough, capable, honest, and determined people who enjoy the challenges inherent in pursuing these wary birds. The process itself selects and shapes the hunters. I have devoted entire chapters—Warriors, Native Sons, Only in America, and the four pieces on James—to descriptions of a special kind of turkey hunter, those I call the Keepers of the Faith. Most are not celebrities or CEOs of huge corporations. They are free, creative, honest, and proud Americans. They are representative of the many common citizens of this nation who bring passion and integrity to the pursuit of difficult challenges.

I have not protected the identities of these Keepers of the Faith. With a bit of research you could track them down. The one exception is the character I call "James"; if you go looking for James, you will not find him.

I speak of the special *American* nature of wild-turkey hunting. Not only is the creature unique to the Americas, but the democratic nature of our nation has provided hunting opportunities to members of all socioeconomic classes. You do not have to be rich to hunt the American wild turkey. Among developed nations, it is *only in America* that even the most impressive game can be hunted by ordinary citizens.

Turkeys help keep us honest by providing a pure measure of success. You cannot buy competence at turkey hunting; you cannot talk your way into the status of a great hunter, or gain efficiency by becoming a company man, being obsequious, looking good, or networking.

The respect earned by turkey hunters is important to them. Many have derived confidence, self-esteem, and public recognition from their accomplishments as hunters. In many cases these decent Americans were not provided with the educational opportunities that allowed them access to prestigious jobs. By contributing to their self-worth and giving them a measure of public recognition, the wild turkey has been very important to the quality of their lives.

I have tried to capture the spirit of turkey hunting. I have written many stories because it is difficult to understand turkey hunting's appeal unless you are exposed to both the common themes and the subtle differences. I offer examples of the significant variations between spring and fall hunting. I include chapters—Marathon, A Dagger in the Back, The Fall Experience, The Spring Experience, and The Toughest Game in Town—that speak to the special character of the hunting.

Any turkey hunter can make the disastrous mistake of placing too much importance on killing a bird. Two chapters, Terror and The Trap, describe how that can occur, and the potentially catastrophic impact it can have.

Hunters also do foolish things in the field. Examples of the turkey-hunter-as-clown are provided in several chapters. My partner and I are prominently featured in these episodes. The fact that the dedicated hunter is ready to do just about anything to kill a turkey can result in some rather amusing experiences. Take a look at Houdini, The Importance of Turkey Calls, Butterball, Partner, Camouflage, and Turkey-Hunting Fatigue.

There are also stories about the companionship generated by turkey hunting. I love to hunt alone, and many forms of turkey hunting are well suited to solitary pursuit; still, the bonds formed between hunters are strong. The chapter on my relationship with my partner is important to me. Turkey hunting can bring together people from very different backgrounds and subcultures. I address this subject in the chapters Diverse Backgrounds—Common Obsessions, and Only in America.

One of my goals in the book is to contribute to increasing the status of the American wild turkey. This great creature has still not received the respect it deserves. A critical reason is that most people equate the turkey with the domesticated bird raised on farms. It is important that the world knows what a special creature the *wild* bird is. Many chapters here articulate the case for the wild bird, but it is the entire thrust of the chapter In Praise of the American Wild Turkey.

A number of the stories speak to the sacred nature of the places we are privileged to hunt. Great hunters love the areas they frequent. One chapter, Carter's, is named for property I have hunted for more than twenty years. I try to communicate how important it is to me. In Sacred Places in the Promised Land I look at the vast areas all Americans have to enjoy. I make the point that each of us has an obligation to invest time and money to protect the still-wild places we enjoy.

I hope my respect for women is obvious in a book that is dedicated to a subculture dominated by males. I am the father of two daughters for whom I have unlimited admiration and respect. My wife is my best friend and the person I admire most in the world. My chapter Nell is an important part of the story of my own turkey hunting. My wife has been at the core of my success. Many great male turkey hunters have women in their lives who have made it possible for them to commit the time and effort required to become successful. In many cases those women have made significant sacrifices to allow men to hunt—or, more accurately, to hunt with passion and intensity. As a teacher, I have quietly cheered for all the women who entered the male-dominated Washington and Lee University at which I have worked. Many Keepers of the Faith are cheering for women as they attempt to achieve some measure of equality. I hope this is read by aspiring female turkey hunters, and I wish them the best. I will be thrilled by their successes.

A number of pieces address the question of why hunting is so captivating to contemporary humans. We do not reap economic gain from our hunting, yet, our commitment of time and money to the chase can be extraordinary. Why? In a number of chapters—including The Seed, Escape, The Passion, The Pure Measure, and Beginnings—I examine that provocative question.

I hope the stories will feed your desire to hunt wild turkeys. The hunting can add excitement and fulfillment to your life. It may be a modest adventure by the standards of some human endeavors, but it has provided great thrills for those of us who are not climbing Everest or sailing around Cape Horn.

IN PRAISE OF THE WILD TURKEY

Many eloquent hunters sing the praises of upland birds. They call the ruffed grouse king. They love the bobwhite quail and proclaim him the southern gentleman's bird. They describe the superb sport the woodcock provides for close-working dogs and quick-shooting men. They write of the ring-necked pheasant, claiming that this arrogant and adaptable immigrant will be the upland king of the future.

I believe the wild turkey deserves the title King of the Uplands. He has great credentials but has received relatively little acclaim. Why? The answer is simple. Few turkey hunters are eloquent. The poet can fit his grouse into rich afternoons that precede productive evenings of writing. The turkey hunter's full day leaves no time or capacity for eloquence in the evening. He moves to bed at an early hour, his body numb with the fatigue that the demanding day has conferred.

Historically, the case for the wild turkey is strong. The pre-Columbian American Indian perceived the turkey as king of the upland birds. It was the turkey—not the smaller gallinaceous birds, the grouse and quail—that was worshiped in the religious ceremonies of Native Americans.

It was also the wild turkey that attracted the attention of the Spanish explorers. The smaller grouse, similar to the red-legged partridge of Spain, did not impress the Spanish—but the turkey was different. The bold, proud conquistador enjoyed the bold, proud gobbler. To have suggested to either the American Indian or the early Spanish explorers that the wild turkey was not king of the American uplands would have been ludicrous. At an early stage in the history of the United States one of America's great minds, Benjamin Franklin, suggested the wild turkey as an appropriate symbol for our country. In 1776 the suggestion was viable; today the idea would be met with laughter from most citizens.

The wild turkey is a victim of the interest he stimulated during the earliest periods of European settlement of the New World. The domestication of the turkey was an economic success, but a catastrophe for the status of the great bird. The sleek, beautiful, wary creature of the wilds evolved into the fat, ugly, stupid butterball of captivity. Nothing speaks more powerfully to the need to maintain wild areas, and the great animals those areas nurture, than the contrast between a wild and a domesticated turkey.

It is hard for me to see domesticated turkeys being carried to market. They are jammed into cages so small the birds cannot stand. Along the road you will see the bodies of a few that were jerked out of their pens by the wind while in transit. I have seen them hanging in the slaughterhouses, waiting to be killed. All my anti-hunting friends buy the neatly packaged breasts in the markets. I wonder what they would do if they were forced to watch the obscene slaughtering process. The killing of a wild one is so much more dignified and humane.

The wild turkey provides the greatest challenge that upland hunting offers. No other upland bird is as strong, fast, elusive, tough, wary, or clever. The difficulty inherent in killing a mature gobbler is sobering. If it were not for the existence of the spring season, when the bird is often blind with virile lust, mature gobblers would rarely be killed. I challenge anyone, from any part of the world, to name a game animal more difficult to hunt than a mature wild turkey gobbler in the fall of the year. Do not try to make a case for "dangerous" game. If you want to face true danger, don't waste your money going to Africa—just drive one of America's most dangerous roads on a regular basis. The killing of most dangerous game with a modern rifle and a guide is less challenging, and less dangerous, than killing a quality whitetail from a high tree stand. I know guys who have hunted dangerous game in Africa and Alaska. I have yet to meet one who could cope with the challenge of mature fall gobblers.

The wild turkey is a remarkable biological construct capable of incredible physical feats. A turkey can flush with incomparable violence and thread his way through dense cover. In another setting, the same bird may leap off a ridge and sail across a valley with greater speed than a driven pheasant. A grouse might fly three hundred yards on a long flight; a wild turkey will fly three thousand. No bird in the world combines such powerful flight with comparable running speed. No imagination is so vivid as to provide an accurate picture of a healthy turkey sprinting across open terrain. The speed contradicts his anatomy.

The first time I saw a gobbler make a long flight, it scared me. He flushed off the mountain, beat his wings twice, and glided over the valley. My stomach became light as I watched. The last time I had felt anything similar was when I had watched small dots fall from a slow plane. Each dot was a friend, and it was several long seconds before the parachutes deployed. The gobbler didn't belong up there, either. It was too high for something that large. Unlike the guys over the Fort Bragg drop zone, however, the gobbler was in command of his descent. I watched him glide over the dark woods, the light fields, the shining river, and lost him when he blended into the distant blue ridge. I don't know how far he went, but from the topographical map, I calculated he was two thousand feet above the river. At that altitude, with his size, someone should have seen him on a radar screen.

Once my partner and I were trying to stay focused after an arduous day of searching for fall birds. It was roosting time, and we were straining to hear the often subtle sounds the birds will make going to the roost. Both of us flinched when the sound waves hit us. I have never heard a Patriot missile fly overhead, but the rush of air must be comparable. The sound shattered the quiet woods. Then we saw the gobbler heading toward the distant interstate. He looked as if he were locked on a target. Put six-foot wings on a bowling ball, drop it from four thousand feet, and let it pass within a hundred yards—and you might duplicate what we heard. As I watched the turkey sail toward I-64, I wondered if an eighteen-wheeler would disappear in a fireball.

Despite his size, the turkey's coordination and grace can be astounding. If you doubt the coordination, watch one sneak through the woods. Every step the turkey takes is deliberate; often, one large foot is held up in the air for long seconds before it is put down.

If you have been impressed by the pheasant's ability to hide, I hope you have an opportunity to watch a twenty-pound gobbler stretch out flat in minimal cover and disappear from view. I once saw a flock of twelve birds disappear in six-inch-high corn stubble.

The turkey is also capable of almost noiseless flight. Although it is true that a gobbler can crash through brush with an explosive power that makes the flush of a grouse seem tame, the same bird can pitch off his roost and glide to the ground without a sound.

Many tales have been told about the visual acuity of the wild turkey. Any hunter quickly learns that a turkey can see into all but the most impenetrable blind. Even experienced hunters will be baffled by situations in which they sit motionless in a good blind, and an approaching turkey will flush for no apparent reason. In such cases it is no doubt the bird's incredible vision that has identified something unnatural.

The hearing of a turkey is as keen as his vision. The caller's softest yelp will often stimulate a gobbler on a distant ridge. Frequently it will be hard for the hunter to believe that the distant, barely audible, gobble is in response to his call.

The turkey's endurance is challenged every year by winter storms. I have stepped out of my house into the violence late at night and wondered how the birds could stay on their wind-lashed limbs. Somehow they do.

The immensity of the challenge provided by turkey hunting is compounded by the difficulty in cleanly killing this great creature. Walk up to one after he has been immobilized by your shot, and his courage will be painfully obvious. The largest bones in his body smashed, his muscles torn, he will hold his head high and his eyes will remain defiant. The strength and tenacity of a mature turkey are awesome. Many men respect the pheasant for its ability to survive grave wounds and elude a retriever. The pheasant is indeed a tough bird, but a turkey is much more difficult to recover. If you think a wounded pheasant is elusive, wait until you have to chase a crippled turkey. A mature gobbler will outrun a pheasant the way a cheetah would outrun a bobcat.

No turkey is equipped to inflict serious injury on a human; however, a mature gobbler can look threatening when he comes to your call. His head is huge, and his eyes burn as they search the area. The turkey may not be armed, but his body language is that of a warrior.

A wild turkey has the capacity to lift the spirits of those of us who love him. I remember a day when I needed to see one. I had had a distasteful interaction with an administrator and was desperate to get into the hardwoods. I was angry and disturbed as I drove away from the town. The walk in the forest with the great dog helped, but it was only after I saw the two gobblers on the logging road that I felt renewed. I watched them at a distance of two hundred yards until they sensed my intrusion and were gone. Still, seeing them restored my courage and spirit. I remembered a comparable experience in Washington, D.C. I was there to attend an anthropology meeting. I watched young graduate students play posturing games, and I listened to the tedious papers. One professor was going through the usual endless slides when a picture of a naked woman flashed up on the screen. It had been placed in the projector by his students. It is the oldest gimmick in the game, and it put me over the edge. As I left the meetings, I could feel my impatience and anger. The traffic on the Beltway didn't help. I had stopped at a traffic light, wondering if I would make it back to my hotel, when I heard Canada geese calling. I looked up and saw them—a small flock two hundred feet above the noise and congestion. They looked so elegant and noble. The wild birds got me through the weekend.

Wild turkeys have a presence. One evening a friend and I were perched on the roof of an old cabin that overlooked several fields. It was almost deer season, and we were hoping to see a good buck. Our patience was rewarded when one drifted into view. We watched the deer with the detached attitude of avid wild-turkey hunters. We were trying to assess the buck's antlers when a mature gobbler marched into the field. We instantly stood up and lost our coolness: "Look at him! That gentleman owns Waynelee's field. I mean, he flat *owns* it!" If a Cape buffalo had walked out of the hardwoods, we wouldn't have been more impressed.

I once read a story about Al Davis, the owner of the Oakland Raiders football team. He had gone to scout a college running back, but his attention had been drawn to a different player, a freshman quarterback who walked with a slouch but had a *presence*. Davis said that Joe Namath's presence "tipped the field." A wild turkey gobbler does the same.

The wild turkey is a beautiful bird. In assessing his appearance, do not look at the many inaccurate paintings that show the bird with small eyes and short legs. Look at photographs of the mature bird, with his enormous eyes and long, powerful legs. Observe him alive. A turkey loses a great deal in death—the colors fade, the body stiffens, and the head and neck are twisted in grotesque poses.

The calls of wild turkeys are wonderful. From the subtle to the loud, from the musical to the raspy, all are thrilling. The gobble of the male turkey is simply as exciting a wild sound as can be heard in the field—anywhere in the *world*. The impact it has on the avid hunter is profound. This spring, my hunting partner and I were tired from a busy winter semester at the University. The first early morning of scouting was tough. After climbing the steep ridge, we were dragging. When the mature bird gobbled it was as if we had been hit with an electric shock. The call was bold, defiant, boastful, and challenging. It sent a shiver through my body. I could see the comparable effect on my partner. The fact we had both heard hundreds, if not thousands, of gobbles over our many years of hunting did not diminish the fact it *instantly* energized us, and erased our fatigue.

I challenge you to find a creature that has more pride than a wild turkey gobbler in the spring of the year. His pride will get him in trouble, but you have to appreciate the way he feels about himself. The mature gobbler is our most arrogant native son.

The best spring gobbler hunter I've ever met was an eighteen-year-old GI in Paris, when Charles de Gaulle led the Free French down the Champs Elysées. In reflecting on his role as a witness to history, the soldier said, "John, there were grown men and women around me crying. The only other living thing I'd ever seen that had the arrogance and pride of that big Frenchman was a wild turkey gobbler. De Gaulle passed twenty feet from me, and I kept waiting for him to turn toward me and gobble."

This great bird inhabits those precious still-wild places in this country. He lives on rocky, cold hardwood ridges, in damp, warm southern swamps, and on bare, arid western plateaus. He does not accept the alteration of his environment. He is not a bird of game preserves, semi-wild hunting, or backyards. He puts our obligations to our planet in perspective. If wild turkeys were relegated to zoos, our loss would be incalculable. A turkey in a cage is not a wild turkey. This great bird will not tolerate the crimes humans commit in the name of progress. We owe him the good fight to protect his habitat. The human experience creates the opportunity and imposes the challenge. His survival is in our hands.

2

THE SEED

I have always loved to hunt. How the passion was born remains a mystery. Neither my father nor my mother hunted. No grandparent hunted. Many of my male classmates at my tiny elementary school in Bucks County, Pennsylvania, fooled with hunting, but I was the only one *captivated* by it.

The first clue may have been that I seemed mesmerized by wild creatures. When the bold pheasants sprinted in front of the school bus, I was the only kid *thrilled* by the sighting. I remember uttering an involuntary "oh," and sticking my head out the window to watch the birds for as long as possible. My response would elicit teasing from my peers.

Friends have said it was the circumstances that I enjoyed—I lived on a farm—that created the addiction. I do not dispute that it would have been more difficult in other settings, but this is not an adequate explanation. My classmates grew up on farms, but pheasants did not thrill them. Also, Bucks County was not a place that was supportive of hunters. My friends were not the children of farmers, but rather of professional parents who worked in New York and Philadelphia. Unlike my special parents, most were contemptuous of hunters. I remember being embarrassed when my parents' friends learned of my hunting. Many did not hesitate to make it clear they thought the activity was the domain of the cruel and intellectually limited. A parent of a classmate said, "I am so glad David has had no interest in hunting. I know Johnny has asked him to go with him, but David hates killing." To be characterized as someone who "enjoyed" killing was difficult. It would take me a while to figure it out, but I knew early on that my passion for the hunt was not based on a desire to kill or inflict pain. While I was the aggressive hunter on the school bus, I was also the one who grieved if a hen and her brood of chicks were killed by the vehicle. The fact that David had no desire to kill sounded nice, but I knew if every pheasant chick in Bucks County were killed in a hailstorm, David would not care. The tragedy would shatter my world.

There was no powerful hunting subculture that led me to my commitment. In contrast, there was no mystery concerning why I played lacrosse. My father had played at Hopkins, and my relatives—both males and females, and all from Baltimore—viewed the game as inherently superior to all others. I was captured by lacrosse the way a kid from Sudbury, Ontario, is compelled to play hockey. What option does he have? The culture of Canada pushes him onto the ice. There was no such cultural pressure for me to hunt.

Literature was critical in stimulating and feeding my passion. My parents introduced me to Ruark, Faulkner, and Hemingway. I learned of cultures in which hunters were honored. The literature was supplemented by outdoor magazines. I read them all. Vicariously, I went from the savannas of Africa to the ridges of British Columbia as I read every piece that Jack O'Conner and Warren Page wrote in *Outdoor Life* and *Field and Stream*. Since I had no family member to serve as a hunting mentor, the articles were educational as well as entertaining. It was not just the great stories, though; I read all the hunting catalogs, too. I still wonder how many precious parts of my brain are filled with esoteric hunting data—such as the muzzle velocity for every bullet weight, 110-, 130-, 140-, 150-, and 160-grain, that was ever commercially loaded in the .270 Winchester. I had a burning desire to learn as much as I could.

I vividly remember my first kill. It was before I was old enough to go hunting. The game was a large rat our hired man, Willie, had seen by the corn crib. I was nine and my armament was a little pellet gun that was accurate up to about fifteen feet. I built a blind by the corn crib and waited for the rat. Willie saw me in the blind early one Saturday morning and told my mother I would grow tired of waiting before lunch. At dark I returned to the house and told my parents I would get him. They smiled but did not laugh at me. Willie said the rat was too smart to trap or poison and I would never kill him.

I became obsessed with the rat. When not in my blind, I practiced with the crude gun. I baited the area outside the corn crib with grain and told Willie not to go near it. There was no literature on rat hunting, but something told me that I should keep the places the rat used as free from human activity as possible. My first retriever, Dandy, was ready to give up on me—I had eliminated our daily walks to sit in the blind. One evening I heard my father laughing with my mother about their rat-hunting son. My father said, "Well, at least Johnny has shown he has great patience, a trait that should be beneficial later in his life." The old man did not realize it was a *selective* patience. Johnny is the most impatient person his tolerant wife has ever known. Put me in an auditorium, compel me to listen to some phony, and I will go crazy. But put me in a turkey blind and I will not tire—no matter how long the wait. The waiting is not an ordeal, it is a process I love.

One day, well into a week of waiting for my rat, I saw the grass at the base of the corn crib move. I remember trembling with anticipation. When he appeared, my shaking stopped; a warm composure came from somewhere. I moved the gun slowly, picked a spot at the base of his ear, and touched the trigger. A faded black-and-white photo, no doubt taken by my tolerant mother, shows a little boy holding the rat by the tail. My expression is serious. My mother must have been concerned about infection, because a large glove covers my rat-holding hand.

The rat story is important, because it is impossible to use "love for nature" to explain the captivation of that hunt. The barnyard was not pristine, nor was the rat attractive. There was no *need* to kill him. He was doing no damage, and I had no sense of potential health threats he might impose on our animals, or us. The key is: He was *game.* He was clever and cunning and hard to kill under the limitations *I had imposed.* I did not consider the use of poison, or gas, or a trap—those crude, cruel tools were for farmers. I was a hunter. The photograph is of a hunter and his trophy. I knew this was not a forty-inch Stone sheep, but I took the rat fairly.

My success changed perceptions of me. After the kill, Willie was not so quick to dismiss my ideas. My parents let me know they were proud of my accomplishment. *I* knew no classmate would have killed the rat.

My parents not only were tolerant but also helped me find farms to hunt. My father traveled a lot, so my indulgent mother arose early to take me to a new farm. If anyone ever indicated her small son was not worthy of attention, she would step in. I vividly remember one incident. I had gone to Paul Jaeger's wonderful shop outside of Philadelphia to look at an expensive German drilling. I was in high school at the time and looked two or three years younger than I was. When I politely asked one of Jaeger's clerks if I could see the gun, he said, "You can't afford that gun, kid; why waste our time looking at it?" I was humiliated by the comment, and did not reply. Suddenly, I saw the clerk's eyes move from mine to my mother's, and his expression changed. I turned to her and saw why. She moved steadily toward him until her face was so close to his that he pulled back. She hesitated for a second, then said, "Get the gun." We walked out of the store with the drilling. My mother finished the transaction with the clerk without saying another word. The clerk responded to each of her hand signals with alacrity.

My first real game was the ring-necked pheasant. It was easier for me to sleep on Christmas Eve than it was on the Friday night before the pheasant season opened, on the last Saturday in October. The dates of October 26 through 31 became special for me, and I know they will remain so for the rest of my life, no matter how far I am from the fields of Bucks County.

After more than forty years, I can still see the feathers floating against the perfect blue sky when my first cock fell into the corn. It remains the most vivid memory of my adolescence. I was a successful athlete in high school and college, and I received the accolades our culture bestows on those who are coordinated and quick. I threw touchdown passes and scored goals on lacrosse fields. I do not remember the touchdowns and goals; images of the kills in the field are still accessible in my brain.

Early on in my hunting career, I enjoyed the pride of my successes. It made me feel good to hear my father say with some intensity, "I'll be damned, Eileen, the little bastard got another one." My self-esteem was fed at school when, while eating lunch, I heard a classmate say to another boy, "If you go with Johnny, you *will* see pheasants."

I earned respect from not just my peers and family but also adults. The landowners whose property I frequented did not see hunting as an important activity, but most of them registered the fact that it was a rare day when I did not have a cock bird with me when I thanked them for allowing me to hunt. The clear, cold fact circulated: Joe McDaniel's kid consistently killed the wily pheasants.

My successes were privately gratifying. I knew how quickly pheasants learn to avoid hunters, and how few of my friends were successful. I learned that experienced hunters regularly returned from the field without birds. I can remember my sense of accomplishment as I walked toward the house with the warm weight of two pheasants resting against my lower back. A ritual evolved with the fallen birds. I would clean them carefully, stroking their beautiful feathers before placing them in my game pocket. When I killed a brace, I made sure they were balanced perfectly and positioned so that both sets of long tail feathers extended from my jacket.

I enjoyed working hard to master the skills. I practiced with the shotgun until my shoulder was bruised. The wingshooting itself, as an art form, was captivating. No matter how many times it happened, it was magical when the shot intercepted the flying bird. I did not know the distance to the pheasant, or its speed. There was no computer or chronometer built into my 16-gauge Ithaca. I knew scientists needed those tools to direct their missiles to *stationary* targets. All I did was focus on the bird, swing my shotgun, and touch the trigger when it felt right. On a good day every pheasant fell.

I read all I could about pheasant hunting. I kept detailed notes concerning where I found birds, and where they would seek refuge when the hunting pressure became intense. I worked hard to kill game cleanly. Despite my efforts, the tough pheasants occasionally escaped after being crippled. A failure to retrieve a bird was crushing. I learned how valuable dogs were in reducing loss of game, and I was never without one. At times the kennel was filled with them. I loved all the dogs; they enriched my life, that of my original family, and eventually that of the family my wife, Nell, and I established.

I enjoyed the spirit of providing for my family. I was not so naive as to think it was a significant economic contribution, but I knew both my parents enjoyed eating the game. When I told my father I had a brace of pheasants for dinner, his celebration may have been a bit more enthusiastic than necessary, but he *loved* to eat them.

Philosophically, the fact that I loved animals and birds and yet was driven to kill them was always difficult. As I grew older and read the words of others who attempted to address this paradox, I accepted the concept that a love for birds and animals and the passion to pursue them were not contradictory. I did not hunt to inflict pain or see beautiful creatures suffer. I loved it when the shot charge froze the pheasant in the air and killed him instantly. It did not always happen that way, and I was not horrified by the need to kill the bird with my hands. I learned to do it as quickly and humanely as possible, and accepted it as part of the process. In contrast, I was appalled by the obscene "hunting films" that showed game being shot in slow motion. I did not hunt to watch animals suffer and die.

My hunting instead provided me with wonderful images of wild creatures. The pheasants at the Philadelphia Zoo were dull in color, and their feathers, and spirits, were broken by the cages. When the keepers threw grain into their pens, they ran to it like chickens. The pheasants I flushed in the cornfields were wild, competent, and challenging. Each thrilled me in a special way. The memories of specific birds has remained with me. Even in distant retrospect the details are still vivid. With one I see the sun highlighting the myriad colors of the feathers, with another I hear the arrogant, defiant, raucous cackle.

The passionate hunter becomes intimate with his game, and that intimacy brings respect. You learn how tough, clever, and courageous the creatures are. Your admiration and respect for them finds expression as you keep images of them close to you. My childhood room had no picture of my hero, Joe Namath, but it did have pictures of pheasants, and a ceramic vase with a tail feather from every one I killed.

My love for the field established a philosophical orientation that was removed from Christianity and closer to that of hunting cultures, which revered wild creatures and saw killing as natural, death as inevitable. The Sioux did not read Darwin but, unlike Christians, would not have seen his theory as threatening. My beliefs were not popular. Crazy Horse would have understood. The local minister, the Reverend Dr. Brown, did not. My evolving philosophy may have helped draw me to the crosscultural respect that is at the core of anthropology.

Many have suggested that companionship is the reason we hunt. I loved to hunt and fish *alone*. It was hard to find peers who took it seriously enough. My dogs never tired of the chase; my young friends did. I cherished the freedom my independent orientation gave me. Many experiences seemed appropriate only if undertaken alone. When I found the spot where a buck had left his sign, I never considered going back with a companion. Part of the thrill was going out into the darkness alone and finding my way to the remote location. I would wait for him in the cool, quiet, secluded place—alone.

Despite my solitary pursuits, I did benefit from mentors. One was a gunsmith who provided counsel in his shop. A second was a housepainter who took me beyond the confines of the neighbor's farms. Neither man would have suggested he sowed the seed in me; my passion was there before they provided their support. They corrected my mistakes, provided guidance, and tempered my excesses. I wanted every tool that would help me meet hunting's challenges, so I was a sucker for any gimmick in the catalogs. My mentors did not eliminate my excesses but they did help impose a measure of control.

I remember when hunting helped me during tough times. I was a lucky young man who knew no family tragedies; however, I had my setbacks, and I recovered and regained my spirit in the field. As I grew older and the challenges became more formidable, the escapes gave me strength.

Those who have been close to me have reflected on what it was that fed my passion. My mother said it was my love for nature. A fascination for the natural world was an important part of it, but I knew it was more complex. I loved animals, birds, and fish; however, simply observing and studying them was not enough. I needed to *hunt* them. My father thought it was the same competitive drive that also attracted me to team sports. The problem with his explanation was that so many of my most competitive friends had *no* interest in hunting. Nell celebrated my intensity and passion and articulated the theory that predatory instincts were a part of my being.

I do not have the answer. It is with no false humility that I say the appeal remains a wonderful mystery in a life made richer by the thrill of the chase.

3

BEGINNINGS

My first memories of wild turkeys are from the occasional stories about them that I read in outdoor magazines. I enjoyed the pieces, but my interest was tempered by the sense that I would never have the opportunity to actually hunt these birds. I read in the same spirit with which I read about African game. The swamps of the Deep South seemed as remote as the savannas of Africa. There was a chronological component to the remoteness, too. Unlike many of the African stories, most of the turkey-hunting tales were set in the early twentieth century. I remember looking at old photographs of southern hunters. These black-and-white prints showed guys in antiquated clothes, often standing next to vehicles, each with a shotgun in one hand and a huge gobbler in the other.

I first hunted turkeys when I was in college, and the experience was a debacle. It involved a day of aimless, unproductive wandering in a section of national forest a native had told us held wild turkeys. It would get better—but it took a while.

There were two more significant commitments in my life to complete before I had the time to develop my hunting competence. The first was an eight-year quest for a Ph.D. in anthropology at the University of Pennsylvania. After that ordeal, I faced another hurdle: two years' active duty in the army. Toward the end of my army career, I was asked to return to Washington and Lee University in Lexington, Virginia, to teach anthropology. I did not accept the job solely because of the growing turkey population in western Virginia, but I was aware of the hunting opportunities.

The fall before I began to teach, I decided to invest some of my army savings. The idea of stocks and bonds seemed sterile, and I was able to convince my adviser, my father, to allow me to buy land in the West Virginia mountains. It would be accessible from my new job, and had the potential for appreciation. And at seventy-five dollars an acre, even my education in anthropology did not keep me from seeing it as a lock. It was not coincidental that the area held wild turkeys. There was even a little cabin on the property. Early release from the army allowed me to plan a weeklong hunt there. After fourteen-hour days in both graduate school and the military, the idea of a week to hunt seemed too good to be true.

After I was discharged, I returned home to plan this special hunt. My parents understood my strange priorities and were supportive of my plans. I had had plenty of time to stay in shape in the army, so I was not worried about the physical challenges of the fall hunt. However, I had great doubts about my ability to cope with the birds themselves.

I wasn't worried about my gun, though I had bought it after college when an area near our Pennsylvania farm had been designated "buckshot only" for deer hunting. The gun was a classic—an early three-inch Model 12 Winchester with a thirty-inch full-choked barrel. I was excited about trying large turkey shot in it, and I peppered my crude, homemade turkey targets with the big Number 2s.

The maps depicting the ridges and hollows were also exciting. Still, my father began to raise questions about the mental health of a young man who—after release from two years in the army—spent his evenings reading topographical maps and practicing with a Turpin-style yelper. This was before the era of instructional tapes and videos. I read and reread the simple directions that came with the call, and hoped the sounds that were driving my parents crazy would fool a turkey.

The literature on wild-turkey hunting was limited in the 1960s. It consisted of a couple of classic books, which were primarily oriented toward the spring season, and a few short paperbacks on general hunting techniques. I read and reread the material.

Finally the chosen week in October arrived, and I put all my gear in my old jeep and headed toward the hills of West Virginia. The trip to Elkins was instructive. The mountains that had appeared so inviting on the maps looked much more formidable on the ground. The sobering challenge of finding the birds in the vastness of this wilderness left me feeling hopeless. I needed to talk to the forester who had arranged to have trees planted on the property I had purchased. He was very kind and rekindled my enthusiasm by telling me there was a state park near my land with large bird populations. He asked if I had any maps, then laughed at the large inventory I offered. One did cover Kumbrabow State Park, however. With this forester's help I looked at the roads and determined which areas might be best. When I left his small office, my enthusiasm was back.

In my little cabin that evening, I tried to plan the hunt for the morning. The topographical maps reduced the area to clean lines, showing none of the dense thickets of laurel and hawthorn I had seen on my short scouting drive into the park.

In the predawn darkness, it was the unknown I faced as I gathered my gear and headed out toward the vehicle. As I drove through the tiny town of Valley Head, I reflected on the week ahead. I felt some trepidation. I was too young and bold to recognize the risks involved in climbing into the mountains alone, but I noted a general uneasiness about riding away from the lights of the town. I passed no vehicles on the highway, and it was not long before I pulled off onto a rough road that followed a small stream. The road was in terrible condition. Jouncing in the vehicle was no fun, and I wondered if I would even be able to reach the place I planned to hunt. I can still remember the intensity with which I gripped the steering wheel as the vehicle crawled up the hollow. I stopped once to try to orient myself. It had all seemed so obvious as I looked at the friendly map in the cabin the night before. With less-than-supreme confidence I put the map away and prepared to hold my vehicle on the road. At one point I encountered a puddle that looked extremely deep, and I wondered about the wisdom of pressing on. I stayed on the edge of the drop-off, and the jeep crawled out.

When I saw the pull-off I was ready to stop, even if I was not precisely where I had planned to be. It was a relief to get off the terrible road. I saw that the hollow was broad, and I knew that if I climbed it and headed north, I would reach the main ridge. I took a rough bearing with my compass, collected my gear, made sure I placed my car keys in a safe place, and started to climb.

I was a long way from the ridgetop when the first light filtered into the hollow, and I picked up my pace. Sweat ran down my face. When I finally crested the ridge, I looked back into the hollow and beyond and saw the many ridges that reached into the dark valley. It did not escape me that the vastness of the country would make locating a flock of turkeys a challenge.

Each distant ridge was a distinctive shade of black silhouetted against the slightly lighter sky. The stars were bright and the cool air tasted pure. It was so different from the farmland I hunted in my youth. The big woods thrilled me.

As full light came, I saw deer sign everywhere on the high ridges. The sign was similar to what I had seen on the farm back in Bucks County, but the hardwoods were different. Yes, the huge oaks and hickories were familiar, but the big black cherries and beeches were new to me.

I found myself enjoying the flora. The trees were spectacular. I was awed by their majesty. The smells of the big woods were different; there was a rich musklike odor, for instance, that I assumed was a product of the many decaying leaves. At times I entered stands of conifers, and the smell of pine was wonderful.

On the downside was the fact I did not see much mast. The only acorns I saw looked old. I was eager to find turkey scratching, but in the first two hours I didn't see anything to indicate a turkey had ever been on the mountain. By the end of the long day I still had seen no sign.

Nevertheless, I enjoyed the mountains and returned to my car tired but excited about the fact that I had more days to invest. My reading had prepared me for having to work to find birds, so I felt no sense of frustration.

I realized just how tired I was when I cooked my meager meal on the camp stove. After dinner I played with a turkey call for a while, but it was not long before I was ready for sleep. The luxury of being able to go to bed at nine o'clock escaped me.

My second day was no more productive than the first; moreover, the strain of the hunt was beginning to have an effect. There was no calling practice in the evening. When I hit the cot, I was asleep within seconds.

I was beginning to appreciate just how tough this game was. You had to hunt all day. The hunt was not broken up by a pleasant ride in the car or a relaxed lunch with other hunters. You were alone on some high ridge when you ate your meager lunch and planned for the long afternoon. Yet the arduous nature of the hunting had an appeal. It was like the sheep hunts I had read about. I expected to invest significant time. I liked the process of searching the big woods. The fact that I could hunt all day without seeing another person was a new experience, and I liked it. The physical demands of the hunt were obvious. There was something captivating about the tremendous challenge.

When I finally saw the sign, I wasn't sure it had been made by turkeys. It looked like what I had read about in the books, but I was almost afraid to define it as real. The small areas that had been swept clean of leaves were much neater than areas that had been pawed up by deer in their search for acorns. I found turkey droppings in one area that had been scratched, and the excitement ran through my body. My search became intense. I followed the sign for only a short way before it gave out, but it was all the incentive I needed. My afternoon went quickly. When I climbed into my vehicle at dark, I was proud of myself for sticking with it. I decided to reward myself with a meal at a small diner.

When the waitress brought me the menu, she asked if I were deer hunting. I told her, "Turkey hunting," and she said, "That explains why you look so tired." Later in the meal she told me her husband had killed an eighteen-pound gobbler the year before. I said I had never killed one but was excited by having seen some sign. When I walked up to pay the man at the register, he surprised me by saying, "I hear you found some sign." When I answered in the affirmative he added, "That's good to hear, because no one has been seeing any." As I left the tiny restaurant, he wished me luck as if he meant it. I had been defined as a turkey hunter, and I liked it.

I never found the flock. I never saw a wild turkey. I did, however, enjoy the hunting. The birds introduced me to their magnificent country, their incredible elusiveness, and the sobering challenges of hunting them. They were *big* game. You carried a shotgun, but this was not bird shooting: The only hunting as challenging as this involved creatures twenty times larger than a wild turkey that lived in the remotest places in the world. A few were capable of killing you. None generated more passion in their hunters than the birds that had eluded me on the rugged, remote ridges of West Virginia. I had not solved the problem of finding them in the big country, but the message of how special they were, and how difficult the hunting was, had been learned—and I would not forget it.

I had not yet become a member of the subculture of turkey hunters—that would require an apprenticeship—but I sensed how special the group was. It was clear that this type of hunting was not for the easily discouraged.

I drove out of the dark hills eager to return. From that critical week on, wild turkeys have occupied a part of my brain. In spirit, they have been with me, and an important part of my life, ever since.

4

FALL FREEDOM

The dark hills were silhouetted against the slightly lighter sky as I pulled onto the logging road. This leg of the trip was rough, and I braced myself in the seat as the bouncing headlights cut through the trees. Finally, I reached the area from which my hunt would begin. Stepping from my Wagoneer, I was invigorated by the mountain's cool air. I closed the door of the big vehicle with care to avoid the loud, metallic sound.

Despite the lack of light, I was comfortable and relaxed as I set out on the familiar trail. My clothes fit perfectly, the gun was familiar, and my boots had logged miles on these ridges. The smells of the November woods, the strength of my body, and the expectations of the day surged through me. It was great to be on the mountain!

I walked through the dark woods toward the big hardwoods near the head of the little cove. I had seen fresh sign in this area two days before, and hoped to get lucky. As dawn came, I listened for any sounds of birds leaving their roosts, but none were forthcoming. I began the arduous search. There were no shortcuts. I climbed up and over ridges, and down into basins. I disciplined myself to approach each ridge with caution and to examine each hollow. My legs began to ache and, despite the forty-degree temperature, sweat rolled down my face. I hunted hard all morning and was satisfied.

There was no time for the grouse hunter's relaxed lunch on the tailgate of a station wagon. There was no playing with a warm and happy Brittany after lunch. As a turkey hunter, you open your modest lunch on a high, hardwood ridge overlooking a spring. You are *still* turkey hunting. You need every minute, every day, if you want to be able to kill them with the consistency that separates the Turkey Hunter from the good old boy who blundered into them.

I planned the afternoon hunt as I ate. It was warmer now, and I decided to work down along a stream that drained the mountain. It was almost 3 P.M. when I finally reached the valley. I bent to drink from the small stream, confident that there was no threat of pollution here, back away from the roads, the cattle, the quail, and the quail hunters. Drinking from clear streams is one of the fringe benefits of turkey hunting. After a brief pause, I continued.

The sight of a small circle of earth devoid of leaves sent a shiver through my body. My entire being tightened as I inspected the sign—fresh! The scratching was indicative of a large flock. I moved quickly, aware that the birds could be close. My body drank the adrenaline and I acquired new strength. I paused, and now I heard them raking the leaves. I judged them to be seventy-five to one hundred yards downstream. I moved carefully. The knowledge that I would get close to them increased the thrill. The laurel opened a bit, and I saw them. My mind raced to assess the situation. Was I close enough to rush? Would it be better to try to circle in front of the feeding flock? Had they sensed my presence? A *putt-putt* alarm call answered my questions.

I threw myself toward them. My sprint was the infantryman's rush, hampered by equipment, the mobility of my arms restricted by the heavy gun. I had rushed this way not long before carrying an M16. I expended no more effort then than now. The birds lifted their heads quickly, their eyes focused on the awkward, onrushing predator. Their small brains identified the image as a threat, and they leapt into flight. The flush of one turkey is impressive; the flush of a large drove is pandemonium. Birds I had not seen before materialized suddenly, and the six became twenty. All were airborne at the same time. Sometimes one turkey responds more slowly than the rest, but not this time. Their flight was not graceful, yet in a very short time the very large birds had climbed through the trees and were out of range. Incapable of any more productive action, I watched the birds fan out in flight, each seeking its own path of escape. The surprise, and the dense cover, resulted in effective dispersal of the drove. Scattered!

I sat down to collect myself and plan a strategy for the next episode. It was three-thirty, and I doubted that the birds would try to get back together before sunset; still, I would wait until dark. I constructed a blind in the precise spot from which the drove had flushed. I climbed in, allowed my tired body to sink into the cool soil, and waited. Sunset came quickly, with no indication that a wild turkey existed within five hundred miles. I began the long walk back to the Wagoneer. As I walked, my mind drifted to the scattered young turkeys on the mountain, eager for the companionship the drove offers.

In the warmth of our home Nell listened to her turkey-hunter husband's story and asked, with a smile, "You wouldn't be going up there tomorrow, would you?" I smiled back.

Despite my nine o'clock bedtime, I was tired when the alarm rang and moved to the kitchen with determination, if not grace. A quick breakfast, a relatively short ride in the vehicle, a long climb through the dark woods, and I was back in my small blind. I eased myself into a comfortable position and waited for dawn.

As the first hint of light came I huddled against the penetrating cold, yet enjoyed its stimulation. My down jacket provided its special kind of warmth, and I felt comfortable in circumstances many of my associates would see as inhospitable. I loved the insulation the remote place conferred. Trees took form as the light of dawn gently entered the woods.

I was tight with anticipation, because I was sure there would be turkeys calling on the mountain. The wait was short. The call was clear and unmistakable. It was the high-pitched whistle of a young turkey, and the thrill of hearing it was tremendous. I knew I had to make a good response, and this challenge was heightened by my knowledge that the young bird would probably come running. My hours of practice with the call and successful experiences in the past gave me confidence. I put the small diaphragm caller onto my tongue and placed it against the roof of my mouth. I prepared my throat and mouth, and then expelled three quick bursts of air from my lungs. The young turkey answered immediately, and I sensed an urgency in his call. I prepared to respond, but the call of another turkey, also below me but farther to the right, interrupted me. I answered, and both turkeys screamed back. The bird to the right called again, and this time he sounded closer. I called back, trying to interject a sense of urgency into my notes.

It was a thrill to hear the bold, loud calls. The second bird came steadily toward me, and I shifted my position in anticipation. I listened intently to his call, picking up the characteristic deep yelps with which the young gobbler terminated his *key-key* call. At a range of what I guessed to be a hundred yards, the bird let out a series of loud whistles. I pushed my gun forward until its blue rib and tiny bead of silver were superimposed on a tangle of laurel. I focused on the small bead, the laurel blurring into an impressionistic pattern of color. I heard the distinctive two-footed gait as he came. His approach was anything but stealthy. I moved the safety off and searched frantically; his steps were so loud I could hardly believe he was not visible. My first glimpse was a flash of black to the right of where I had focused. I adjusted my body slightly and looked down the rib of the shotgun.

At fifty yards, the entire bird was visible, his body iridescent in the now-higher sun. He came boldly, long legs reaching forward, the bright eyes burning with intensity. The tiny silver bead entered the bright picture, and I placed it under his head. The bird kept coming. He was close enough. I felt the gun jar in my hands before I had made any distinct decision to shoot. I refocused my eyes after the recoil and saw the broad, red-brown tail fanned gracefully in the air. It was enough. I jerked myself from the confining blind and ran, on cramped legs, to the dying turkey.

I was pleased to find that I had killed him cleanly. Tiny points of bright red blood marked his head. I inspected the wounds, and then looked at the bird. The dark feathers were brilliant. I was particularly impressed by the size of his eyes. I sat back and enjoyed the warm satisfaction of the moment.

Turkeys *can* be killed by chance, but when they are killed consistently luck has nothing to do with it. I celebrated my victory with a can of Coke, unashamedly proud. I gave humble thanks for being provided with the opportunity. I admired the wonderful bird and enjoyed my own company. Finally, I put the turkey's legs together, grasped them tightly in my right hand, swung him over my shoulder, picked up my shotgun, and headed down the slope.

I have never had much trouble carrying a turkey out of the woods. I've killed a few large birds—one weighed in excess of twenty-two pounds—but the walk out has always been easy. The joy of victory is a great antidote to fatigue.

I moved easily through the woods with the large bird on my shoulder. When I reached the logging road, I transferred the turkey to my other shoulder and headed toward the vehicle. I couldn't wait to show it to Nell.

I heard the pickup struggling up the road before I saw it. It lurched into view, its metallic colors and harsh noises obscene intrusions on the serenity. Three large men struggled to stay in their seats as the vehicle fought up the difficult slope. As I moved to the side to let them pass, I pulled the turkey up a little higher and tried to look nonchalant. The hunters didn't pass. Three heavy men descended from the still-moving car to see my bird. They had on new camouflage gear, and their guns were unscarred. None had ever killed a turkey. They, too, were free to hunt turkeys for the first week of the season. The fatigue of the day and a half they'd already spent in the woods was visible in their faces. The men pressed close to examine my young gobbler. They asked the inevitable questions and then squeezed back into the pickup, their spirits and strength renewed. I watched their heads bob in animated conversation as their truck surged up the road. They were confident, *too* confident. As I watched the vehicle struggle, I smiled to myself. Somehow I knew that my turkey would be the only one taken from the drove on that still-young fall day.

5

PARTNER

I like the word. From a historical perspective, it is associated with the American West and the bonds formed among those facing the formidable challenges of the dangerous country. A partner was someone you could depend upon. The relationships were important and enduring. Comparable bonds exist between good friends who hunt together.

Fall hunting is particularly conducive to establishing a close partnership. Spring turkey hunting is a solitary game, but in the fall you are working with flocks that can provide multiple opportunities. More important, in the fall you must find birds that are elusive and silent—an arduous task made easier by the cooperation of partners. The area one person can cover in an afternoon or day is severely limited; however, intelligent planning can allow two of you to make more comprehensive searches. Also, from a psychological perspective, knowing that your partner is working hard to find the flock is an incentive to your own attempts. I search with more diligence when I know Gary is out there, charging up the ridges and searching the hollows.

Unselfishness is critical to great partnerships. You must see your partner's accomplishments as equivalent to your own. At times the unselfishness a partner will demonstrate sets a standard that is hard to match. Let me describe one example. This experience involved a good friend whom Gary and I had invited to hunt with us. He is an avid hunter, but has only one leg. On the first morning the three of us were in a blind hoping to call up a bird, with no success. Since our guest was not able to move with any speed, he and I stayed in the blind while Gary left to search for the birds. He found and scattered a flock at two-thirty that afternoon. He was a good thirty-minute walk from us, and we had no idea he had found birds. Moreover, Gary had to attend a wrestling practice at four o'clock, and had very little time to get back to the car and drive to town. Many men would have convinced themselves that to be able to make the practice they would have to leave immediately; the flock might still be scattered the next morning and available for them to call. What Gary did, however, was *run* the long distance back to our blind. My guest and I both killed birds I called up that afternoon while Gary, who had given us this opportunity in the first place, was working with his wrestlers. Our kills significantly reduced the chances that Gary would have any opportunities the next day. For him, the unselfish partner, that was no problem.

One great advantage of having a partner is that he may be able to search for the flock at times when you cannot. If your work schedule makes it impossible to get out in the afternoon, your partner may be able to go after the birds. There is no question that the opportunities to find birds are more than doubled with a partner.

A partner can also help you find new areas to hunt. For the solitary hunter there is a tremendous temptation to simply stay with properties that have been productive in the past. With a partner, you're much more likely to reach out to new horizons.

A partner is a tremendous asset in keeping you focused when things get tough. It takes discipline to sit in a blind when there is no indication that any birds are listening to your calls. It is significantly more challenging to muster that discipline if the weather is bad. You are much more likely to remain committed if your effort is mirrored by your partner.

One of the most sobering experiences for any responsible hunter is losing game. A partner who brings a fresh and calm perspective to the search for a crippled bird can mean the difference between success and failure. In our twenty-two years of hunting together, I can think of at least four instances when Gary's contributions made a difficult search more effective. We didn't succeed in finding the injured game in all of those cases, but our partnership allowed us to intensify our search.

But partnership is more than just pragmatic. Friendship is at the core of the partner relationship. Sharing stories is a wonderful part of enjoying the hunt. Gary and I enjoy talking to each other about past hunts and anticipating future days in the field. Our conversations are relaxed, interesting, and often filled with good-natured teasing. Their frequency and duration are testimony to the value we place on them.

A partner needs to be a good listener. We have often reflected on the fact that some friends who hunt with us only want to tell stories and are never interested in what we have to say. It is gratifying to be listened to. Gary and I have been through years when one or the other of us was not in the area. We both agree that during these times, our hunting was not as enjoyable, because we missed sharing the stories. It is no coincidence that our success during those years was usually less than what we experienced together.

A partner is a wonderful tool by which you learn, too. Two hunters obtain much more data than one. Discussion between hunters is a key to learning, to figuring things out. The frequency with which committed partners communicate about hunting would be incredible to many nonhunters. Nell frequently teases, "Has Gary called yet tonight?" The question is reasonable, because at the height of the season we talk at least once a day.

Partners can find a lot to laugh about. Gary and I have sometimes taken inexperienced hunters with us whose comments still send us into fits of hysteria. One was the Ph.D. who asked us if "the bucks were the ones with horns on their heads." Another was the friend whom we put on a stand. He spent the entire day walking around the tree trying to stay warm. When I saw Gary that evening it took him several minutes to gain control of his laughter so he could tell me about the deep path the guy had cut into the soil in his continuous march around the tree. The final comment that Gary struggled to offer, between his laughter, was that the guy said, "I can't understand it. I didn't see a thing all day."

Then there was the time the macho friend came upon us just as we'd killed one of our largest deer ever in Virginia. When the guy asked us how much the handsome buck weighed, we guessed between 150 and 170 pounds field-dressed (in fact, it weighed 148½). He said, "I can carry that all the way back to the car on my shoulders—no problem." We let him try.

Another story involves a character who has been known to us as "Noodles" ever since the episode. It seems that this guy was having trouble hitting a large cardboard box at a distance of about twenty feet with his "deer" rifle. The gun was an old World War II military rifle from Italy. It had a military peep sight, which our friend thought was the source of his accuracy problems. He told us he "couldn't see enough" through the sight, so he decided to *drill* it open to see more. His crude effort did enlarge the aperture, but after the alteration he missed the box by even more. He decided he had gone too far with the drilling. As we waited to see how he intended to put the metal back, he came up with a brilliant idea: "A common noodle will fit in the now-larger aperture." He ran to the kitchen of the hunt camp, found a can of Chef Boyardee's finest, and was thrilled to discover a noodle did fit snugly into the bored-out peep sight. He returned to the "range," squinted through the crooked noodle, and shot. As a hole appeared in the upper edge of the large box, the man's howl of delight reached through the entire camp. Gary and I ran from the scene trying to control ourselves until we reached the seclusion of Gary's cabin—where we collapsed and laughed until we cried.

We also enjoy laughing at ourselves, and have had many opportunities to do so. In the earliest stages of our turkey hunting careers we made some incredible errors. Several were what we call the "early '70s mistakes." Each of us has a favorite. Gary's is from his first spring hunt. He took his new box call up a steep ridge where he had been told a gobbler resided. Sure enough, at first light the bird was not far away. Gary had heard that concealment was critical, so when the turkey gobbled, he decided to lie down behind a huge fallen oak. With his face pressed into the ground, Gary heard the excited gobbles coming closer and closer. Soon he heard, for the first time, the sounds of the bird going into strut. His thrill of having the prey so close was tempered by the realization that his chances of killing the bird were slim if he kept his face pushed into the ground. Gary lifted his head and stared right into the bark of the huge oak, which was four inches in front of his face. Meanwhile, the confused turkey gobbled from directly on the other side of the tree. The idea of leaping up to surprise the bird seemed foolish, so Gary spent the better part of an hour staring at the tree, too close to be in focus, inches in front of his face. Finally, the love-crazed gobbler had had enough of the teasing hen and walked off, still gobbling. Gary pulled himself out of his "blind." Lesson number one learned by the Blind Partners: Never hide so well that you are not able to see the bird.

My own early '70s mistake involves a basic personality flaw. When I first started reading about turkey callers, I was fascinated by a piece on the traditional suction-operated yelper. These wooden, flutelike calling devices were patterned after the early wingbones. I found them fascinating and decided to try one, even though the literature warned against starting out with this type of call. My pride drove me to take on the challenge. I would master it with hard work. I knew that I was avoiding the callers that were deemed good for a beginner, or easy to use. I *was* a beginner, of course, but I didn't want to be defined as such.

For three years I used the yelper. Oh, I called a few vulnerable birds, but it wasn't until I admitted that my calls did not sound as much like turkeys as those being made by the simpler boxes and slates that I decided to try the other calls. My stubbornness had clearly kept me from selecting the most efficient tool. Gary still laughs about "the Doc's first call."

As we grow older, there are more things to laugh about. As a result of our shooting, we both have marginal hearing. We have tried all the aids. They do amplify sounds, but they also have the unfortunate attribute of making it difficult to determine where the now-louder sound is coming from. This is especially tough in the spring season, when you must determine the location of the gobble: If a bird sees you before you see him, your precious opportunity will be lost. Gary and I call ourselves the "deaf squirrels." I coined the title when I watched Gary scramble around the base of the tree he was sitting up against as he frantically tried to determine the direction a gobble was coming from. He looked like a very large, hyperactive squirrel. I have done the same thing.

Just last year Gary scattered a flock of turkeys only half a mile from me. Despite the fact we made contact on our small radios, we could not find each other. We spent an entirely frustrating two hours trying to find landmarks we could both identify to allow us to get together. The pathfinders failed.

A partner is there when you are both facing tough times. When the motor on your boat gives out, you can pool your poise to address the potentially dangerous situation. Gary and I have talked under the pressure of a storm moving in when we were in danger. The fact the two minds are focused helps. We have not had to fight our way out of a dark urban street, and I hope we never will, but if I ever am in that situation, Gary is the guy I want next to me.

A partner is an invaluable source of constructive criticism. For example, it is not easy to assess how a call sounds if you are making it. A partner can comment on its quality, though, and contribute to your developing skill. Many inexperienced hunters will—with honesty—rave about your calling. An experienced partner can provide more measured comments.

The most important time to have a partner is when things are not going well and a word of support is critical. For the support to be meaningful, it must come from someone who cares. A great partner takes enjoyment from your success, even when it is not being mirrored in his own hunting. In such a relationship, the success of your partner becomes analogous to your own. In essence, all accomplishments are shared, because you have developed your skills together.

Another key ingredient in a great partnership is trust. There is a wonderful ease with a partner. You learn what to expect from each other, and there are no surprises. I am relaxed when I hunt with Gary—and there are very few other people with whom I can relax when hunting. I have good friends who scare me to death when they have guns in their hands. The problem is simple. Most American hunters have had very little training or experience with firearm safety. If you are an experienced hunter, you no doubt have some frightening stories to tell about carelessness with firearms. One of the joys of hunting with a partner is that you can trust him totally.

Trust and honesty go hand in hand. I draw great strength from the fact that when Gary says something, I can accept it without question. I am not talking about blatant dishonesty, but the kind of exaggerations that so many people indulge in. When your partner tells you that a flock contains eight to twelve birds, for instance, you do not have to invoke some equation to reduce his estimate to realistic numbers. Because so much hunting strategy is based on information about flock activity, you have to be able to depend on the quality of that data. Any experience with a person who has a proclivity to exaggerate will tell you all you need to know about the importance of honesty.

A partner encourages you to do bold things. I am sure Gary and I would not own the range of equipment we do without the support, both financial and psychological, that our partnership provides. It is so much easier to buy the new decoys when your partner is ready to help.

I've almost learned to expect Gary's humility when he discusses a time he has screwed up an opportunity in the field. Unlike so many folks I encounter, he is not afraid to say, "I had a great chance and just choked it." He readily admits it when he does not know something. This humbleness is a product of his pervasive honesty.

I see him as the quintessential American. A product of the heartland, he grew up on a farm and took advantage of every opportunity he was offered. He would have done his part on any of the distant battlefields, but he was not born at the right moment. He has traveled, and athletes from other cultures have been exposed to his wonderful mixture of competence, humility, good humor, and kindness. I can easily imagine him teaching skills to young wrestlers in Istanbul. He would be intense and patient, kind and persistent. He would work as long as they had the strength to continue. After practice, he would have a beer or two with them. When he left, you would not be able to convince any of the wrestlers that Americans are bad guys.

6

IN PRAISE OF THE WILD TURKEY HUNTER

The wild turkey selects his hunters. The chosen combine physical toughness with intelligence and determination. One superb turkey hunter I know is a native West Virginian who speaks with a soft mountain accent. His career, forestry, allows him to be close to the birds he loves. During last year's spring season James had thirty days to hunt. He went twenty-eight times. On each of those mornings he was up at three-thirty to face the demanding hills of eastern West Virginia. He is an accomplished caller and splendid shot. Last spring he failed to kill a gobbler. He was neither surprised nor distraught.

In many small mountain communities, the respect the turkey hunter earns cuts across sub-cultural boundaries based on sex. I have heard his proud wife or mother say, with unusual boldness, "James hunts nothing but turkeys; he doesn't fool with anything else." Mountain women boast of men who kill turkeys consistently.

Wherever he is, whatever the cultural situation, the turkey hunter is in a class by himself. He enjoys this status in the warm den of a prestigious hunting club or a tiny barbershop in a bleak Appalachian town. You do not become a turkey hunter by virtue of killing a turkey, because turkeys often fall to deer and squirrel hunters. You acquire the status of Turkey Hunter by being *consistently* successful. And to do this you must develop a degree of specialization. It is nice to talk of how, in May, you can hunt turkeys in the morning and fish for trout in the afternoon; if you expect to kill your gobbler, you will fish very little. You must invest full days for consistent success. The 2:30 A.M. alarm will dampen the enthusiasm with which you await the 3:30 P.M. hatch of mayflies. The turkey asks a lot. The true turkey hunter pays his dues.

You must have endurance. I have hunted turkeys with accomplished college athletes who suffered under the strain. James was no longer young when I started to hunt with him, and he amazed me with his stamina. It was not a competitive drive he displayed. He did not try to run up the mountain to show he was in better condition than I; he just kept going. He did it every day. If you wonder what the rigors of a sheep hunt are like, try a turkey in the rugged ridges of our Appalachian states. If you kill grouse with your legs, you kill turkeys with your heart.

The grouse hunter will assert that his bird also demands dedication and hard work. Which is true, but the distinguishing element is the level of patience required. The grouse hunter may wait hours between flushes, but he rarely goes for days without seeing game. The turkey hunter develops the quiet dedication of the Atlantic salmon angler. Both are addicted to the pursuit of the difficult. The nature of the game—be it salmon or turkey—provides you with the strength to face the incredibly long periods between encounters with the quarry. Even the most avid grouse hunter has difficulty being satisfied on a day when he fails to flush a single bird. I submit that this difference is a measure of the superiority of Atlantic salmon to other fish and the wild turkey to other birds—even ruffed grouse.

One of the most important turkey-hunting skills, the art of calling, was first practiced by American Indians thousands of years ago. There is nothing to indicate that a turkey can be fooled more easily today. On the contrary, there are those who would suggest that the challenge has dramatically increased with greater hunting pressure. Contrary to what turkey-call salesmen may assert, it is not easy. James is a great caller. He is accomplished with many different types of calls. Despite his skills, he still works at it. He believes that you *must* work at it.

James is also a great naturalist. Part of his success in the field is based on his knowledge of the flora and fauna of the areas he hunts. He *knows* where turkeys live and what they eat. He has learned how they avoid predators. He has filed all the data in his brain. He never stops trying to learn about the wild turkey.

The turkey will not be consistently harvested by poor shooters, because the vulnerable parts of the bird are small. If you use a shotgun, the turkey will teach you the modest range at which such a weapon is lethal. If you ever read about eighty-yard turkey guns, rest assured that the author doesn't know how difficult a wild turkey is to kill. You can quote pattern densities all day, but any turkey that is more than fifty yards away from you has a good chance of surviving your shot regardless of gauge, choke, load, or shot size. If you live in a state in which rifles are legal, you will learn you have to be able to shoot with great accuracy to kill turkeys consistently. My partner and I believe rifles should not be legal, because the chances of crippling a turkey with one are so great. The modest skill that many efficient deer hunters find adequate will not be good enough.

James would be quick to tell you how often the great birds elude him. It is the toughest of games. James celebrates the difficulty. His personality does not demand daily success. The magnitude of the challenge is at the very core of what he enjoys. If I were asked to characterize James with one word, it would be *perseverance*. He loves to stay after the birds when the going is particularly tough.

If turkey hunters have a weakness, it is a proclivity to avocational arrogance. The respect we allocate to hunters of other game is usually measured. Deer hunting with a firearm for any legal animal is perceived as an activity best suited to adolescents, the out of shape, and the old. Asked once, "Why don't you hunt deer?" James raised his light blue eyes to the interrogator and said:

> If he has some time, any fool can kill a deer every year. He just finds himself a trail, sits down, and sooner or later some impatient fellow from the city will chase one up the trail. The deer won't see him and its mind isn't quick enough to convince it what to do about the boy's smell. So the deer gawks at the smell and stamps its feet. Now if that good old boy doesn't get too nervous he will fill the shaking scope up with the large vital area of the deer, jerk the trigger, and kill it.
>
> A turkey hunter, don't you see, he goes out and *hunts* a turkey. He doesn't depend on tree stands, or drives, or long-range rifles. He also isn't going to find his game in the backyard or a farmer's field. A turkey hunter has to be *smart enough* to know where the flock will be, *tough enough* to get to them, *clever enough* to put his blind in the right place, and *talented enough* to call a bird. Now, after he has done all that, he better know how to sit still and be patient. Finally, when the bird is there, he better shoot *straight* and *quick*, because a turkey's head and neck are small. Even a young one won't stand there gawking at you and stamping his feet.

7

WARRIORS

For our proud Plains Indians, warrior status was achieved by displaying exceptional courage. Today the opportunity to ride with the world's finest light cavalry may no longer exist, but there remain warriors in our ranks. I write about warriors because to be a *great* turkey hunter, you must be a warrior. I am not so arrogant or poorly informed as to suggest that you must be a turkey hunter to be a warrior. Many domains afford the opportunity to become one.

Many of our greatest athletes have earned the title Warrior. They have gained this recognition by performing at a high level under great pressure or when in pain. Striking images come to mind: One is of Chuck Bednarik, the last N.F.L. player to play both offense and defense. He is walking out of Franklin Field in the mist of a cold November day in the 1950s, his face bloody and his uniform dirty and torn. He does not look like the statue of the Greek athlete. His appearance is more in keeping with the disheveled GI holding on to a tiny sliver of beach at Normandy. It is the look of the warrior.

The warrior athlete is the aged Archie Moore fighting when he was too old to be in the ring. He was knocked down early in his bout with a young Canadian. I was a kid when I watched Moore on the black-and-white TV, the referee counting over him. My father said, "Too bad, Johnny, Archie was a great fighter. I am sorry you have to see him go out like this." Somehow, and for reasons known only to warriors, Moore got up at the count of nine. Forty-odd years later, when I can no longer remember the year of the fight or the name of his opponent, I can still feel the thrill that ran through my preadolescent body as I watched the middle-age black man refuse to stay down. I vividly remember recoiling when my father screamed, *"Hold on, Archie,"* and the tightness in my body as I watched Moore fend off the young man for two more painful rounds. In the next my father said, with feeling: "Archie is straightening him up with his jab!" Several draining rounds later my father and I jumped from the couch screaming as Moore caught the kid. My mother ran into the room to find out what was happening.

My examples are both of the stereotypical *male* warrior athlete. I stand by my choices: Bednarik and Moore were warriors. Still, they had a large stage on which to display their courage. In our culture this stage is rarely provided for women. To me, one of the most exciting aspects of turkey hunting in the 1990s was the growing number of women participating in it. I believe that many women warriors will be selected to hunt turkeys.

Diana Golden Brosnihan provides a picture of the warrior woman. She was an athlete who battled cancer with a courage that left witnesses breathless with respect. One catastrophic setback after another did not stop her. I never saw her perform; I learned about her from a wonderful article by Harvey Araton in the *New York Times*. A small photograph showed the still-brave eyes and the effects of the terrible disease. I read this fine piece at a time when I had just learned I faced two more operations—my sixth and seventh—for skeletal problems that had plagued me for the past ten years. I was feeling sorry for myself until I saw what the gallant woman had faced in comparison.

Anonymous warrior women are found in many settings. In America they are standing in front of the grim homestead on the prairie with their vulnerable children. They are the ones who got us across the plains—not the gunfighters, but the mothers who would not let their children die, or did not let the death of one keep them from caring for the others. The warrior woman is also the contemporary urban mother who protects her teenager against the gangs, or the woman in suburbia who has a daughter with anorexia and does not cave in.

Conflict and competition are not the only circumstances that spawn warriors. Warriors maintain high standards of performance in every workplace. They are there to stay the course when others take the easy way out. It is the warriors who establish records for not missing days, or coming back quickly after illness or surgery.

Some warriors set standards that few of us turkey hunters can measure up to; to be a great turkey hunter, however, you must be tough. Turkey hunting selects for warriors. You must have tremendous stamina in the face of long odds, physical challenges, and disappointments. The early mornings and long days are draining. You can look forward to naps, but they will never make up for the sleep you miss by getting up at 3:30 A.M. Physical exertion is a factor. Terrain differs, but all turkey hunters must cover ground. In most cases, it is tough.

The season, be it fall or spring, is long. It becomes a marathon. This is not a quick weekend of intense sport—the season wears you down. The length of the spring and fall seasons convinces many hunters that turkey hunting just is not to their taste. It may be that spring mornings are too warm, or that trout fishing is too much fun, or—I love this one—the lovesick gobbler is at too much of a disadvantage.

The warrior tries even when he is in pain. To stop because of a minor health problem is not an option. I could cite cases of hunters who continued despite significant physical problems. Also, unlike the unquestionably tough professional athlete, the turkey hunter does not have highly-paid physicians in attendance. I recently heard two television announcers talk about the unbelievable toughness of a "warrior" who was playing with a bad shoulder. At the precise moment that this praise was being heaped on the running back—who was surrounded by two $350-per-hour physicians—a friend of mine was sitting in his modest home and nursing a leg that caused him so much pain he could not sleep. He could not afford to go to a physician. I met him driving out to hunt two days later. My friend's toughness, and that of many men and women from lower socioeconomic settings, goes unnoticed.

The warrior is rarely found in the luxury lodge where you will see the well-dressed weekenders who shoot geese out of heated blinds or ride horses after pen-raised quail. These men usually dress better, have more lucrative jobs, and enjoy higher status in the community than most dedicated fall hunters. Few of them are warriors.

Warriors rarely use guides. Find a great turkey hunter and ask him if he is booking a guide for his next hunt; you will probably be met with a stare of disbelief. Have you seen many outfitters advertise fall turkey hunts? The reason you don't is that the game is too tough. Spring hunts can be set up for the fat client, but the fall is too demanding. The intelligent outfitter knows that it will be exceedingly difficult to recruit participants if they are told what their chances of success will be with old gobblers.

The warrior is frequently uncomfortable in the macho deer camp, where male bonding often takes precedence over a determined yet quiet quest for competence. Most warriors are not looking for companionship and find the banter of the group tedious and irrelevant to the reasons they hunt. For many in the hunt camp or at the lodge, the hunt is not as important as the companionship, fun, and escape from social circumstances.

The selection process for warriors *is* democratic. The wild turkey is a great equalizer. Education, wealth, and social status all mean nothing. The guy who works the shift at the mill has the same opportunity to hunt turkeys as his friend in the front office. Part of the reason is the extraordinary access to hunting that public property provides in the United States. Unlike the case of upland birds and waterfowl, the large tracts of timbered land in our national forests offer superb wild-turkey hunting for anyone with the toughness to get away from the roads.

There is no occupation or socioeconomic class that warriors cannot come from—but there is none that guarantees membership. No part of the country, no particular ethnic group, is more likely to produce a warrior. Some are the products of the most difficult social circumstances; others have been born to great advantages. There is simply the wonderful common denominator that those who become warriors do so by displaying a profound toughness and determination to succeed.

Can you tell if someone is a warrior by appearance or demeanor? It is exceedingly difficult, but I believe there are some clues. There are not many obese warriors. They work too hard to get fat. They come in all sizes and shapes—and some are big and thick—but not many are "soft fat." A great many are lean and wiry. Some look strong, others do not. If there is a physical key, I would say it is intensity. All the warriors I have known have had it, and you can often see it in their eyes. The best ones have a little of the predator in them. The hunt is not relaxing. It is demanding. The enjoyment comes not from "fun" but from doing a difficult job well.

Perseverance is a key. The turkey-hunter warrior brings an almost compulsive determination to the pursuit. Since most of us are not professional turkey hunters, we have to schedule our hunting around work and commitments to our families.

Warriors are aggressive. They are not abusive, but they do not enjoy failure and are ready to take chances to succeed. Of the turkey hunters I have known whom I would call warriors, few allow themselves to be stopped from getting a bird. At times this aggressiveness can produce ethical challenges. If a warrior hears a turkey just across the property line—not from a sanctuary, but from on another property—will he resist the temptation to go after the bird? I don't think so. Don't misunderstand me; these guys would never consider baiting a turkey, or shooting one out of season, or going onto *posted* property. But they *are* aggressive.

I would be remiss if I did not point out that there are warriors in other fields of outdoor pursuit. Any dedicated hunter or angler willing to endure hardship and put in tremendous effort can achieve the status of warrior. But a lot of turkey hunters are warriors, because the game is so tough. You do not have to be a warrior to shoot doves. It is just a relaxing afternoon of shooting. It is too easy.

The toughest warriors may be the oldest. I love old warriors. I think of the faces of some I have known. When the images of these men come to my mind, they are not in heroic poses—but pride and courage are there. Often they are looking directly into a camera lens, and you can sense the confidence and toughness.

Even today, with field sports still dominated by men, warrior anglers and hunters are not always male. One of the most impressive I ever met was a petite American fly fisher who stalked New Zealand trout with burning passion and incredible competence. She has become a legend among the macho Kiwis, who now call her a warrior.

We need warriors. We do not need them to kill turkeys, but the toughness they develop in the field can pay dividends in other domains. We need them to stand their ground when the ruthless must be stopped and when standards must be set. We need the examples they set each day by refusing to quit, making the tough call, and staying the course despite the odds. They are the ones who will lead us through the darkness.

8

THE FALL
EXPERIENCE

The November evening was cool, and I rushed to feed the dogs. The cold silenced the backyard. "I will need the down jacket in the morning," I thought as I ran my hand through the coat of my strong Chesapeake, Sage. I walked quickly back to the house, shivering with both the excitement of the cold and the knowledge that a scattered flock of young turkeys will be spending a lonely night on Hog Back Mountain.

I had scattered the flock with my setter late that afternoon. I was grouse hunting during the first week of Virginia's combined grouse-turkey season. Every grouse hunt provides an opportunity to scatter a gang of turkeys. If I can, I know I'll have a wonderful chance to call turkeys the next morning.

Back in my home I called my partner, Gary, to inform him of my successful afternoon and its exciting implications for the next morning. When his familiar voice said hello, I answered with a triumphant "bingo!" It is a code we have developed that means we have scattered them. We both laughed. Gary's first question went to the heart of the situation: "Was it a good scatter?" I said, "I think it was. I only saw five, but it was thick, and the contour could have kept me from seeing others. At least two birds went down the mountain; the others went to the north along the contour." Gary asked about the composition of the flock, and I told him it was a gang of immature turkeys—I had found young-bird droppings. Pragmatic considerations—how early we would have to leave, who would drive—brought the conversation to a close.

"I'm going out in the morning," I said to Nell, who responded, "My boy will be a cold turkey hunter." I placed my cold-weather gear beside the door, then went out into the yard to talk to Sage, who would share the blind with us in the morning. She was slow coming out of the house but quick to put her head in my hands. I talked to her in soft tones while the other dogs barked jealously. The cold pushed me back indoors to the sounds of my family. For a short time I joined my younger daughter in teasing her older sister about an alleged boyfriend. Nell soon called the girls to bed; I turned the television to ESPN and endless college basketball. I enjoyed Dick Vitale's hysteria for several moments, but soon found my thoughts turning to the birds. I picked up an old wingbone and was soon lost in calling.

When I awoke, I could feel the cold through the window. I pulled on the soft polypropylene and moved from the room. Nell whispered a sleepy "good luck" as I started down the stairs. Before turning any lights on I walked out into the darkness, felt the cold, and looked for signs of wind. There were none. The thermometer read twenty degrees, which is very cold for the James River Valley.

I drank a cup of coffee and waited for Gary. The small town was quiet and I appreciated the noise insulation the early hour conferred. Gary's car was loud as it pulled to a stop. I got up quickly, glanced around the room, and walked out into the darkness. There was no need for a greeting as I loaded the gear into the car. Gary helped me without speaking, as he has done countless times before. I went back to get Sage, who had heard me and was waiting eagerly. Her excitement was contagious and I smiled as she pulled me toward the car. Gary said, "Well, Sagie, are you going to try to eat a turkey the way you ate that dove?" Sage responded by jumping up and licking Gary before lunging into the vehicle.

We drove through the deserted town. The conversation on the trip to the mountain was between two good friends who are very comfortable with each other. We talked a good bit to the excited Chesapeake, who knows we respect her. There was a lot of teasing and a spirit of relaxation.

Young turkeys are fun, and all three of us were in the mood. The trip was not long and soon we were arranging our gear for the twenty-minute climb. The cold was invigorating, and we quickly arrived. Twenty years of experience made it unnecessary for us to talk. I pointed to the spot the birds had flushed from, using my hands to describe their direction. Gary and I put our packs and guns down and moved out to find blind materials. The Chesapeake got in our way, but we tolerated her playfulness. Streaks of light were visible in the east by the time we put on our heavier clothes and positioned ourselves in the small blind. Sage was not satisfied with the space we allocated to her, and I pretended to be mad as I tried to confine her. We would have at least a twenty-minute wait. I looked at the distant lights of the small town and felt the anticipation.

Gary and I both know there is no such thing as a sure thing with wild turkeys, but a well-scattered flock in the fall is as is close as it gets. While we did not say it, both of us would be surprised if we did not have the opportunity to kill a bird. Yes, sometimes a "sure thing" ends in us not hearing a sound, but such instances are rare. We have never determined what the causes of these disappointments were. In some cases I suspect we made a mistake in identifying the composition of the group: A large flock of old gobblers will not respond to young-bird calls. Another possibility is that the birds had an opportunity to get together before dark and left the area. Finally, we have wondered if some disturbance after darkness, such as raccoon hunters or nocturnal predators, could have driven the birds from the area. Despite the occasional disappointments, though, we expect to hear young birds calling at least eight out of ten times, and to actually call them in to the gun about six out of ten. Many times an old hen will compete successfully with us in calling her brood.

As light entered the forest, dawn came without a sound. The Chesapeake reached up to me with her paw, and I put my hand on her head. All three of us waited.

When features in the woods became visible, I pulled the wingbone from beneath my jacket and put it into my mouth. We were not waiting for an exciting gobble; I would probably begin using the wingbone before we heard a call. I waited several more minutes and finally decided it was time. My soft, grunting tree call sounded loud in the quiet woods. There was no answer.

Gary and I are accustomed to waiting. While cold, it was not painful. Twenty minutes after first light I prepared to make a call that would imitate a bird leaving its roost. I took out the Morgan tube and placed it against my lips. This call was louder, and I heard myself take a breath after finishing the sequence. There was no answer. Far below us we heard a vehicle and human voices. It is always a shock to recognize how far some sounds can be heard. I waited another ten minutes and then made a series of *key-key* runs on my call. There was no answer. We waited. Neither of us expected it to be long.

When the sound came, there was no question what it was. I looked to Gary and he pointed in the direction from which he thought the call came. I nodded in agreement, and we both adjusted our positions. Sage began to shake with excitement; I had to grab her muzzle so she could not whine. There was some tension now with the knowledge that a turkey was coming. I thought my call sounded good, but the quick answer of the bird was reassuring. I turned to Gary, who smiled back. I would let the bird make a few more calls before I responded. The bird called regularly. It was hard to resist the temptation to respond to each one. I called again, and the bird responded immediately. I saw Gary adjust his gun, and I moved to look down the rib of the big 10-gauge. There was no need to discuss who would shoot first: Our policy is to give the hunter who found the flock first chance.

By now my initial nervousness was over and I was beginning to enjoy the aggressive calling. I tried to imitate the tone of the young bird and put a sense of urgency into my calls. Gary leaned over to me and said, "Only gobblers, right, Doc?" I smiled back. Our philosophy is that we should kill only young gobblers. It is legal to kill hens, but selecting gobblers is beneficial to the population. We began this policy in the 1970s and have tried to maintain it. It was easy to do in the mid-1970s when turkey populations were high and there was little competition. More recently it has grown much more difficult. In some years, when the end of the fall season approached, we have been unable to resist the temptation to kill a hen. If one of us does, the teasing imposed by the other is harsh. Now Gary was enjoying the fact that I was avoiding a quick shot at a hen. Knowing it was unlikely that the eager birds would not come to us, Gary leaned over to Sage and said, "If the boss is too hungry to wait for a young gobbler, I would refuse to retrieve it, Sage." Sage was much too interested in the intoxicating sounds coming up the mountain to turn her bright golden eyes to Gary.

Suddenly there came a loud *key-key* from directly behind us. I looked at Gary and we both turned toward the intruder. Our movements were neither graceful nor calm. Experience has taught us that the second bird we hear is more apt to come within range first. The new bird made a long series of whistles and I tried my best to imitate it. Despite the cold, I felt the sweat roll down my face as I worked with the call. I was uncomfortable in my new position and tried to adjust so that I could shoot when the bird arrived. The next call from the new bird was much closer, and I realized that my movements to get into position had become frenetic. The excitement was pervasive and, as Gary and I moved, Sage began to whine. I clamped her mouth and she struggled. The ninety-five-pound dog soon had me in a contorted position and I could see Gary all but hysterical at the spectacle of my wrestling with the retriever. Soon, we heard the sound of bird's footsteps in the leaves. The sounds triggered more adrenaline and my heart began to beat rapidly. I could feel the now-subdued Chesapeake shaking against my leg. Gary glanced at me quickly, and the thrill was obvious in his eyes.

No matter how many times we have the experience, it is always wonderful. Neither Gary nor I has any sympathy for the concept that "calling young birds in the fall is so easy it is no fun." It is inconceivable to me that a hunter would not enjoy the thrill of a young bird suddenly appearing after a protracted sequence of calling.

A sudden movement behind the large oak attracted my attention and I felt my body stop shaking as I watched the bird step from behind the tree. The first thing I looked at was the head. The variation between the head structures of hens and gobblers is a key to sexual identification. This time the large, bulbous head was clearly that of a young gobbler. I heard, or felt, Gary move as I, too, adjusted to bring the gun to bear on the beautiful bird. The young gobbler took two steps, stopped, and then stared at us from a distance of fifteen yards. This was not the inherently suspicious older bird. The jake was convinced another turkey had been calling from our location, and I had enough time to make a careful shot. I placed the bright white bead at the base of his head and felt composed as I touched the trigger. The next thing I felt was the jolt produced by the strong dog as she lunged from the blind. The bird was thrashing on the ground. I knew his head and neck were riddled with shot. The big dog entered the scene and feathers flew as she grabbed the twelve-pound turkey. I placed the call to my mouth and made a quick *key-key*. There was no answer. Gary turned back to the direction from which we had heard the first bird, and I called again. I turned my attention to Sage, who was taking mouthfuls of feathers from the bird. Gary shook his head in mock horror at the less-than-perfect retrieve. I did not want to call the dog for fear of spooking another turkey, so I just watched in some embarrassment, hoping that she would tire of her playfulness.

After longer than I enjoyed, the dog grabbed the bird by a wing and half dragged, half carried him toward us. As Sage got closer, I had the sense that she was beginning to feel some measure of pride in the affair: She lifted the bird higher and strutted toward us. At the blind I took the bird from her, and Gary whispered, "She will eat it if you don't watch her." I smiled and was about to reply when the call of another young bird sent us both into a scramble to reposition ourselves in the blind. Sage looked out toward the new bird with Chesapeake intensity. I began to call with the confidence an already-successful day confers. My calls were loud and bold. Gary raised his head from the stock of his gun, smiled at me, and it began to seem very easy. The next bird came with great confidence. Just before it got within range, yet another bird began to call from the same general direction. Soon the mountain was ringing with the *key-key* whistles of young turkeys. The very volume of the sounds, and the excitement, were wonderful. Enjoying the fact there was no pressure on me, I said to Gary, "You better not kill a hen!"

When the head of the young gobbler popped over the contour, I *knew* Gary would kill him. The bird disappeared at the shot, and the keyed Chesapeake dove down the slope after him.

"Well, I better go and see if that Chesapeake has left any of that bird for me," Gary said. I laughed, hoping that Sage had not gotten too excited. It was not long before the proud dog climbed the ridge dragging the bird. "Good girl, Sagie. Uncle Garo is saying all these terrible things about you and now you make the perfect retrieve." Gary responded, "What's the matter, Sage, has John put you on a diet? John's Chessies always eat at least half of every bird they retrieve."

We compared the two birds in the blind. As always, we marveled at the beauty of these incredible creatures. We soon heard two more young turkeys begin to call. We would call no more birds from this vulnerable flock. Gary and I have no sympathy for hunters who take more than one bird from a flock each. The argument that "you only get a few chances" is phony. If you work at it you will have many chances, and the killing of more than a single bird is abusive. We listened to the wonderful calling for a while, and then left the area so the rest of the flock could get together.

The birds balanced perfectly on our shoulders as we headed down the mountain with the big Chesapeake prancing proudly in front of her two friends.

9

DREAM GUNS

Turkeys have been killed with rifles, combination guns or drillings, and a few with bows, but a tight-shooting shotgun is the turkey hunter's tool of choice. Most experienced turkey hunters have had lifetime love affairs with shotguns. Many of us have vivid memories of times when, as kids, we dreamed about shotguns.

A lot of the dreamers were farm boys. We came from all sections of the country—from the high plains of Nebraska to the rocky coast of Maine. The subculture of the farmer endorsed hunting, and so the primary tool—the shotgun—was in our dreams.

This was before televised sports had come to consume the American male. In the 1950s the New York football Giants' superstar Frank Gifford could go on the popular television show *What's My Line* and stump the panel, because none of the New York celebrities recognized his face. Lots of us played high school football on Friday night, but on Saturday we hunted. For many, hunting became a passion. When I first heard the geese each fall, I would lie awake for hours, too excited to sleep.

Great opportunities were available. Aggressive agriculture had not yet destroyed game habitat. The sloughs were full of water, the fencerows were thick, the poisons applied to control insects had not yet had their catastrophic impact.

The dream guns were the American repeating shotguns produced during the first two thirds of this century. Only the very best made the list. While there might be some debate about those deserving membership, most would agree on Winchester Models 97 and 12, the Browning Auto–5, the Remington 870, and the Ithaca 37.

Only a few boys were lucky enough to start with a dream gun. Most of us invested an apprenticeship on a boy's gun, which was usually a break-open single shot or Mossberg bolt action. At adolescence, we aspired to the dream guns. They were the product of a democratic society, designed by American geniuses such as John M. Browning and built with pride by competent workers. They were made of forged steel with hand-checkered wood; they were efficient and affordable.

The dream guns are an important part of the American story. The Winchester that was taken West to meet the challenges of the wild country was built in the same shop as the repeating shotguns that would dominate the marshes and fields in the twentieth century. Americans had access to double-barreled shotguns, but the repeater was the American gun. One reason was cost. In 1951 the price of a Model 97 Winchester pump was $69.95. The cost of the Winchester Model 21 double, on the other hand, was $298.50—too expensive even to dream about. These were 1951 dollars, remember, and we were accustomed to the disbelief our parents expressed when we stated the cost of even the Model 97.

Other factors contributed to the popularity of the great repeaters. The man who sat in the marsh in Minnesota wanted an Auto–5 magazine full of Number 4s when bluebills came to his decoys—two shells was not enough. The extra shot was critical to the excited Nebraska farm boy who waited for the sprinting pheasants to reach the end of the corn strip and explode around him. In southern Georgia the third shell allowed the bird hunter to establish a reputation for taking three on the covey rise.

Doubles did not enter our dreams, because they were not what our heroes carried. In all my years of boyhood hunting I never encountered a hunter with a Model 21—yet I would see three Model 12s in an average day. I can still see the black-and-white photograph of my favorite outdoor writer, Ted Trueblood, with his Model 12 Winchester in the high Idaho desert. I could not imagine him in that pose with an elegant double. The Model 12 was as American as sage grouse and the high desert that nurtured them.

The durability of the dream guns contributed to their reputations. Farmers and their sons were hard on guns. They were carried in trucks, marsh boats, and canoes. Few were stored in cases. Most stood in the kitchen corner, were hung on pegs on the wall, or were leaned against the feed bin in the barn. We shot farm pests with them in frantic haste before racing for the school bus. We did not find the time to clean them very often; occasionally, our lack of care approached abuse. One man told me how, after losing an oar, he propelled his Barnegat Bay sneak box with the stock of his Auto–5. The gun was not designed to be used as a paddle, but the next day he killed a limit of black ducks with it.

The American advertising industry was young, but the word on the dream guns got out. Traditional ads played a role. We saw the exciting spreads each month in the pages of *Field and Stream, Outdoor Life,* and *Sports Afield.* In addition, there were the shooting annuals, *Gun Digest* and *Stoger's Shooting Bible,* that provided detailed data on the guns.

The most effective advertising was not purchased, however. Each small farm town had its great hunters, and we all knew who they were. More important, we knew their guns. In many areas a great hunter would create a market for a specific type of gun. One of my heroes, Mr. Davenport, used a full-choked 16-gauge Model 37 Ithaca Featherlight. I was not the only boy who aspired to own a gun like Mr. Davenport's.

Histories of the West contributed to the popularity of the dream guns. And we believed all the stories. We would learn that many were more myth than fact, but it made no difference. We wanted larger-than-life heroes and we were never disappointed. Every western film, good or terrible, gave more exposure to gun companies. Is there a former farm boy who cannot conjure up the special script that the Winchester company used for its name? How many hours did we spend turning the worn pages of the old catalogs to look at the dream guns? How many times did we read the descriptions of weights, barrel lengths, chokes, and prices? These were rituals, not fact-finding exercises. It was exciting, and at times therapeutic, to look at the guns, to know they were available, to dream.

The same gun that the hardworking farm boy could afford would also—albeit in a different style—win prestigious shotgun competitions. Until the 1970s Americans were not compelled to import their competition guns from Europe. For the first half of the twentieth century the Grand American Trapshoot in Vandalia, Ohio, was dominated by the dream guns. Today the superb shotguns of Italy dominate competitive events. The idea that a contemporary American repeater could win a major competition would now elicit laughter from knowledgeable shooters.

Dream guns stayed in families. One family I know absolutely refused to switch to the new hammerless repeaters. The Model 97 Winchester—still available in 1951, with its primitive-looking exposed hammer—had been used by three generations of Corrigans. Charles Corrigan Sr. had traded a calf for one in 1903. That gun was still in the family and was accorded a reverence probably comparable to that an Ogallala Sioux held for his grandfather's spear. Corrigans could be identified even before you saw them. Our attention to the guns taught us that the old Model 97s made a unique sound when the pump was activated. Many times we were able to locate Charles Corrigan and his boys in the cornfields by the sounds of their old Winchesters.

Possessions can indicate economic status. Owning a Model 12 Winchester, however—which cost less than a hundred dollars—was not a clue to socioeconomic status; possession of a rel-atively inexpensive gun did not preclude your being wealthy. Many rich men stayed with their Model 12s even when they could afford the world's most expensive guns. This was not an exercise in American stubbornness; on the contrary, many men were clever enough to realize that they would never be able to improve upon the performance of these superb shotguns.

We were told that the English gentry would not welcome the dream guns on their shooting grounds. I do not know if an American ever carried an old Model 97 to the grouse moors. It would make a great story, but I doubt it ever happened. Most of us know the Model 97 Winchester would be out of place in the land of the Purdey, Boss, Greener, and Churchill. I suspect if an American had been invited, he would have borrowed one of the fine English guns and done his best.

Wouldn't it be fun to pick a few of the great American game shots you have known, or seen, to see how they would measure up if they were using our guns? I have my own list of names. No one will have heard of them, but I guarantee that on the grouse moors, the Americans with the dream guns would keep the re-trievers busy.

The democratic nature of hunting in the United States pro-vided opportunities for hundreds of thousands of rural Ameri-cans. Many were blessed with superb coordination and vision. When these requisite physical traits were combined with ample time, lots of game, liberal bag limits, and inexpensive ammuni-tion, the result was a devastatingly effective game shot. The best had a fluid grace, quickness, and ease that had to be seen to be believed. Few of the great ones were ever captured on film, but they remain as part of the legacy of the American hunter. The only way we see them today is in rare black-and-white pho-tographs. These faded photos do not capture athletic skill, but if you look carefully at the faces, you may be able to sense the com-petence and pride. If the hands and forearms are visible, they will be strong and powerful. The body will not be that of a fit-ness fanatic but one that has been toned by climbing ridges, wading swamps, and walking fields.

Memories can be used to create a partial record of the astounding competence of the great game shots. Many of us who were farm boys in Upper Makefield Township will claim, with honesty, that Mr. Davenport *never* missed a Bucks County pheasant. We were all in awe of the fact Mr. Corrigan had, *on more than one occasion,* killed limits of doves without a miss. And we still recollect the incredible grace and speed with which one of these shooters would mount his gun, track a target, shoot, and then move to another bird. The first time I saw Mr. Corrigan take a pair of cock pheasants out the air, I was too impressed to speak. Now more than thirty years later, I can still see the two birds falling into the corn *together.* No athletic feat I ever witnessed in a stadium, or on television, made as much of an impression. Some of the stories no doubt improve with time, but there is no question that the dream guns produced some of the most skilled game shots the world has ever seen.

These guns were built to be sold and cared for in small shops owned and managed by people who cared. Such shops were refuges for farm boys. Any trip to town included a visit to the gun shop. There, the talk was all of guns and hunting. You listened with an attentiveness that only the best of your teachers generated. Some of the finest shops were run by craftsmen—the gunsmiths and builders of the custom guns that became the dreams of successful men. Many were great mentors. We learned not only about firearms but also about conservation and field ethics. Those of us who loved the great small shops miss them terribly.

Women have been conspicuously absent from this consideration of the dream guns. There were women who hunted in the days of my youth, but they were in a minority. Girls on farms were not encouraged to hunt; it was deemed the domain of males. Boys were given toy guns, girls were given dolls. In essence, American cultures determined children's interests according to gender. There were, and are, exceptions to the general rule. Some were famous, like Annie Oakley. The majority of American women who used the dream guns were anonymous; as a boy, however, I knew one. The story was that Mrs. Leydon came from wealth. Her daughter owned a beautiful farm where her grandson and I hunted pheasants. The elegant and tough Mrs. Leydon pursued them aggressively with the only Pigeon Grade Model 12 any of us had ever seen. No artifact attracted more attention from the farm boys of Upper Makefield Township than Mrs. Leydon's Winchester.

The old guns are still valuable today. A clean Model 12 Winchester will bring at least five times its original cost in 1951, simply because there are many who consider it the finest repeating shotgun ever made. Every once in a while a hard-looking guy will stick his head into a local gun shop and say, "You don't by chance have an old Model 12, do you?" The experienced owner will know better than to try to show him what is currently deemed to be "just as good."

Many of us made the tragic error of not maintaining our dream guns. Some were lost, stolen, or destroyed. I had one stolen from the attic of my home. My partner Gary had one taken from his car in Chicago while traveling to the Minnesota farm where the Auto–5 had served with distinction. Both losses were exceedingly hard. To say the guns had sentimental value is to trivialize what the thieves took from us. The guns were important parts of our lives. Gary and I would both go to them to reflect on good friends, great dogs, and the wonderful country at the core of it all.

If the great military victories of the British Empire were won on the playing fields of Eton, America's victories were spawned in the woods, fields, and marshes where farm boys carried dreams guns and developed skills that were relevant to combat.

Today, many Americans lump all those who own guns in the category of violent deviants. The vast majority of those who owned dream guns were not violent men and women. Our guns were not designed for killing human beings. They were made for hunting, and they were used by gentle people who loved animals. Yes, dream guns have been used in acts of violence, but such experiences have been rare. It is true that only a fool would have tried to burglarize a farm on which a dream gun was kept.

The Model 12 with its thirty-inch barrel is not on any list of home defense weapons; but in the hands of a superb game shot protecting his family, it would be a frightening weapon.

My farm-boy friends and I never shot at human targets with handguns. We would regularly throw clay pigeons for each other, and occasionally shoot a round of skeet or trap, but handguns were not part of our world. The idea of shooting at an image of a human being remains as repulsive to me now as when I was compelled to do it in the army.

Our homes never contained assault weapons. I hate the things. They are designed for one purpose: killing human beings. They should be illegal. I still remember when a young man carried an assault rifle into the elegant small shop owned by the great gunsmith George Schielke. Gentle George looked at the kid and said, "Get that thing out of here!"

I love the look and feel of the dreams guns. I took one apart recently, and Nell teased me about the way I handled it. I love taking care of them, handling the rich wood and heavy steel. The receiver of one is silver from forty years of use. The sweat of my hands took all the blue from the gun; however, there is not a speck of rust. From my perspective, it is more beautiful than when new.

I read an article in one of the "prestigious" hunting magazines that has come on the scene in the past few years, and was appalled to see the gun carried by a guy hunting exotic sheep on a remote Asian mountain. This gun had a plastic stock and a silver barrel. I do not doubt that it can shoot, but it is *ugly*. I loved O'Conner's beautiful custom Model 70 Winchester, and Page's 7MM magnum, and Trueblood's factory Model 70. They had a *spirit*.

I remember ordering a custom gun from a barrel maker who had a reputation for building the most accurate of modern rifles. The gun had a wooden stock, but it had been added to the gun by a stock maker in another state. You could tell the gun was built in parts. It shot great, but it looked out of place on the wall next to the dream guns and the rifles built by hand by George Schielke and Julian Nagorski. George's guns always had stocks so characteristic they served as his signature. Julian had wonderful carvings of dogwood blossoms on the forearm and grip. The great makers saw guns as works of art. The spirit of their creations was comparable to that of cane fly rods or osage longbows. The plastic gun carried to the Asian mountain does not deserve to be in the same picture as the magnificent ram.

Americans who owned dream guns have led the fights to protect the American environment. Even before they gained power, the best of the farm boys made efforts. My partner challenged his father's plans to drain the sloughs to provide more tillable land. Gary had never taken a course in wildlife management, but he knew that the birds would disappear if the sloughs were drained. Most of us were not clever enough to see these threats as boys, but a lot of us have tried to help as adults. A list of those who have made the most impressive commitments of time and money to protect areas that produce game will include many who grew up with dream guns. Find the environmental groups that have been most successful in protecting what is left of outdoor America, and you will encounter men and women who came from families that honored the dream guns.

10

THE SPRING
EXPERIENCE

You look at your watch again. It is almost 8:30 P.M., and you wonder where the time has gone. You pick up the phone, dial the familiar number hoping that Gary will answer—it embarrasses you to get Linda, because you call so often. No luck. Linda is, as always, pleasant. You wait for Gary's familiar voice, anticipating the question: "Did you get him?" The answer is, "No. How about you?" Again a negative. It is well into the second week of the season, and Gary's voice communicates his fatigue. The conversation is typical. Each man listens with interest to the story of the other's hunt. A few questions are asked: "You mean where the two streams come together under Piney?" "Was he with hens?" Finally the conversation turns to the next day. You tell Gary where you will go and conclude with a quick, "Good luck." You glance back at your watch and realize you are behind schedule.

The excitement that carried into the evenings of the first few days is no longer sustained. You check your equipment and move upstairs, desperate for rest. Nell is putting the two girls to bed as you enter the room. She says, "Well, I think Daddy might beat my girls to sleep tonight." You smile. You say goodnight, feeling a bit guilty, and head for the bedroom.

It is a "good tired." You know you'll quickly relax into a deep sleep. If every American adult were a spring gobbler hunter, there would be no market for sleep aids. You set both alarm clocks, and check the time—9:30 is not bad. In the instant before you fall asleep you think about the spot you have chosen for tomorrow's hunt. You envision the ridges, the hollow, the small stream, and review the access route you will use. The final picture, as always, is of the great bird.

You rise quickly on the sound of the alarm in the hope you will not disturb Nell. She says "good luck" as you move toward the door. You move downstairs slowly, trying to limit the creaking sounds of the old oak. Each landmark on the short trip to the kitchen is familiar. You speak softly to the retriever, Splash, whom you know is under the breakfast table. The solid thumping of his tail is welcome. The bright light in the kitchen is a shock. You feel pain and move to the sink, fill it with cool water, and immerse your head. The cold takes your breath away, but you feel better as you dry your face. A flick of a switch and the coffeepot begins to make noises inaudible during your loud breakfasts with the family. You take Splash out for a quick walk. The April morning is cool. The stars are bright, and there doesn't seem to be any wind. You become impatient with the dog and pull him back toward the kitchen's bright light.

Sitting alone at the table, you drink the strong coffee slowly. You think about Jesse, who goes every morning without any kind of hot drink, and you wonder how he does it. You realize you are smiling as you reflect on your good friend. You quickly glance at the watch; as always, there is little time left. You go downstairs to get the pack and the gun and to put the camouflage paint on your face. The exercise with the camouflage has become a ritual. You are careful to cover all visible areas. The final step is putting on your boots. It is surprising how many precious minutes you consume with this simple task, but finally you are ready. You make sure the coffeemaker is off, because you don't want to ruin another one. You pick up your pack, gun, and hat, and walk out into the darkness. You open the door of the Wagoneer slowly, anticipating the sound of the latch. You use the parking lights to avoid flashing the headlights on the neighbors' homes. Driving down the familiar street, you glance at your watch—five minutes behind schedule.

The town is as still as it is dark. You pause at the one major intersection as a pickup truck crosses in front of you; a man you do not know smiles from behind his camouflage. You smile back, acknowledging your relationship.

The road is familiar. The drive provides a pleasant rest before the hard climb. You park the vehicle and make sure you have all your gear before you turn to the familiar trail.

The first hundred yards are tough. There is tightness in your legs as you pull up the slope. When you reach the old logging road, your heart is responding to the strain. The road is relatively flat, and your legs begin to eat up ground. You know the route and anticipate the curves that the long-departed loggers etched into the landscape. You are higher now, and there are no lights. You move at your normal pace and enjoy the modest adventure of being alone on the dark mountain. You stop to rest at the long-deserted farmsite, opening your shirt and taking off your cap to cool down.

The interstate is visible in the distance, and you watch the lights of vehicles. A smaller light on a distant mountain calls attention to a hunter who is gaining access. Concerned by possible competition, you look at the closer ridges, hoping not to see a flashlight. There is none. You glance at your watch—late. You readjust your pack and gun and move off.

The last four hundred yards are tough. Your legs ache, and your breath comes in gasps. Finally you reach the spot from which you always listen, then take off your pack and sit down. Despite the cool morning, you are soaked with sweat.

High on a narrow ridge you can listen to four potential roosting areas. There is some breeze, but it isn't bad. If the wind doesn't start to blow, this could be a great morning. You rearrange your gear and button your shirt. It doesn't take long to cool off after the climb.

After making sure everything is in your pack—in case you need to move quickly—you stand up and prepare to imitate an owl. The first note sounds loud and a bit strained. The subsequent notes sound better, and you wait with anticipation. There is no response.

Light begins to enter the woods, and you strain to hear a gobble. Prime gobbling time is about ten minutes away. The minutes pass slowly. Primetime arrives, but apparently no one told the gobblers of Big House Mountain.

He is ten minutes late and a long way off. When he gobbles, you try to determine his position. He helps by gobbling twice in succession. He is on one of the ridges the birds have been on before. It is not the best place, but you can get to him. You put on your pack, grab the gun, and set off down the ridge at a fast trot.

You feel the excitement as you run. He continues to gobble, and each call sends a thrill through you. After two hundred yards on the old road, you turn off to get to the ridge the bird is on. In thicker cover now, you walk at a fast pace, your mind racing as you consider strategy. Finally, you reach the point from which it is possible to get a more precise fix on his location. You stop, your breath coming in gasps. He does not make you wait long. It is a great call—a mature gobble from perhaps four hundred yards away.

It is a favorable situation. You stay well back from the edge of the ridge as you move toward him. A hen calls from below him. He cuts off her raspy yelps with his gobble. Another hen calls, and he double-gobbles. The chorus is a thrill, but the competition is a serious threat to your chances for success. When you reach the spur ridge, he is going crazy. He doesn't sound as if he is much more than two hundred yards away. Should you call from here? Because of the presence of the hens, you take a chance on getting closer. You head down the ridge, not at all sure your decision is correct. You want to stop each time he gobbles, but the calling hens convince you to move on. Finally, at an estimated 150 yards, you stop, locate a nice large oak atop the ridge, and move to it as he and his hens scream at each other. In position, you take out your calls with trembling hands and glance at your watch. It is 6:45 A.M. You decide to use the raspy slate call.

With the shotgun across your knees, you stroke a series of quick, loud yelps. His quick response is thrilling. You touch the big shotgun and make sure you are ready, well aware that a shot might be hours away. You hear one of the hens call, enjoying her quick yelps. There is a good chance he will make some noise coming off the roost, and you strain for the sound. He is gobbling a lot now, and you hope that no other hunter will hear him. Another hen calls from a different direction. The gobbler is playing no favorites. He responds to every call. He sounds ready to accommodate any hen—even the immobile one on the ridge 150 yards above him.

You glance at the watch and, hoping the lustful gobbler will become impatient, decide to wait a full five minutes before calling again. You begin to count his gobbles and lose track at thirty-one. After four minutes you can't wait any longer and hit him with another fast series of yelps. He gobbles back. You relish the tension. You hear his body hit the leaves an instant before hearing the more muffled gobble. He is on the ground. You pull the gun up in the hope that he might try the raspy hen first. Your hope for quick victory is shattered by the loud cutting of one of the hens. The gobbler goes crazy. It sounds as if the two birds are together. There are more loud hen calls, a string of gobbles, and then silence. You try another loud call on the slate, and the gobbler interrupts whatever he is involved with to let you know you should come down to join the fun.

Now what? If you are patient, he might come to you after spending some time with his harem. Your decision is to try to sound like several hens in the hope of attracting them and the gobbler. To implement this strategy, you place all your calls in positions of readiness. You first use the mouth diaphragm, making some soft yelps and a few purrs. This time there is no response. You pick up the small, flat, slate call. The rough texture of the corncob on the striker feels familiar. The yelps from the slate sound good, and you enjoy the very act of calling. The gobbler's response excites you—it is clearly closer. You make several low clucks and purrs on the call, and a hen yelps back. You estimate your distance from the bird at a hundred yards, and you reassess the quality of your chosen position. The ridge is open and wide, and the large hardwoods provide good visibility. It is the type of place the gobbler should come to.

It would probably be smart to let the birds move naturally up the ridge, but you are tempted to play a role in encouraging them. As usual, you succumb to your desire to play an active role and make several more calls. Each time, you receive a searching response from the hens. The gobbler's calls now sound as if he is stationary. You can picture the scene: The great gobbler is going in and out of strut near the middle of the ridge. His movements are graceful, measured, and dignified. There is nothing rushed or aggressive about the display. The hens, probably three or four of them, are close to him but behaving in ways that suggest they are oblivious to his display. You have watched similar performances and, indeed, have yet to see a hen overly eager to mate with a hardworking gobbler. The hens do make the effort to travel to the gobbler, and they do stay with him for hours, but during these extended periods they seem to lose interest in the biological purpose of the meeting.

Imagining the activity just down the ridge, you glance at your watch and realize that the bird has been on the ground for half an hour. Be patient! You know your best tactic is to continue to respond to the hens and try to convince them to come up the ridge with their preoccupied friend. You decide to try the Morgan tube call. The calls sound good, but the gobbler apparently is not impressed.

You consider imitating another gobbler to make the bird jealous, but resist the temptation because your success with the jealousy strategy has been modest. You have not yet tried the old Kirby box. As you prepare to call, you realize how stiff your body has become. Your legs are cramped, and you shift in an attempt to gain comfort. The box feels awkward in your hands as you rehearse the stroking motion. Finally, you let the lid touch the side of the box. The call sounds too loud. You question the intelligence of your choice. A hunter does not get within a hundred yards of a mature gobbler every morning, and it is depressing to think you may have just wasted the precious opportunity. So you quickly stroke another yelp—and this time the great bird gobbles back *instantly.*

He gobbles from the same spot and with the same volume, but you know this is an important communication. The quickness of the reply is not the sole convincing factor. There is an *urgency* in the call. You begin to tremble. You quickly put the box down and move your hands to the cold shotgun. The gobbler aggravates your palsy with two more aggressive gobbles. You know his head is pointed toward you and his small brain is focused. You bring the gun up, place it on your raised knees, and stare down its rib. Your pulse rate doubles. A glance at your watch indicates 7:15 A.M. The woods are silent, and you strain for sounds of the birds. Five minutes pass; your hands tire. The sound of a squirrel bouncing through the leaves hits you like an electric shock.

He gobbles again, but he does not seem appreciably closer. It is time for another decision. He is interested in this hen up the hill, but is he interested enough? Should you call again? You are not sure. Now he begins to gobble again actively, and you perceive that he wants encouragement. He is just arrogant enough to expect this new hen to come to him; all the other girls have! Your failure to move does not make him suspicious, just angry. You can sense the impatience in his gobbles. There is a chance he will come, but you know he may stay where he is, insisting that the "hen" come to him. It is a standoff.

Looking down the barrels of your big 10-gauge double, you feel tightness, anticipation, thrill, and anxiety. "The challenge is to be cool," you tell yourself. This counsel has no more effect than it ever does. If anything, you grow tighter. He gobbles again, sounding as if he is in the same location—a good seventy-five to one hundred yards down the ridge. The next call is that of a hen, and her coarse yelps are closer. She calls again, and you estimate she is fifty yards away.

You debate making another call. The tiny diaphragm is pressed against the roof of your mouth. The hen yelps again, and you call without thinking. Your head bobs as you make the yelps. The gobbler's double gobble generates a fresh wave of excitement. Involved, you make several clucks and purrs on the call, then a series of low-volume yelps. The hen responds, and she is even closer. You look down the ridge, adjusting the position of your body as you strain to hear the sound of the bird, or birds, walking. Seconds race by, and your left leg begins to cramp. The hen makes another call. Your heart is racing now, and while your head is locked in position, your eyes race from one edge of the ridge to the other.

When the rhythmic sound of the walking comes, it is loud and bold. You bring your face down to the stock of the gun. Where is the bird? You begin to wonder if your fix on the sound is accurate, and you lift your face to look just to the right and left of the spot from which it seems to be coming. You begin to panic. If you don't get an accurate fix on the bird's position, you could be caught unprepared. Your new concern intensifies the tension, and you feel your head move slightly. *"Don't move,"* you counsel yourself, trying to remain composed.

Your first clue to the hen's arrival is a flash of black directly above your gun barrels. She sounds much closer. She walks calmly through the light cover of the open ridge. You cannot resist the temptation to watch her for an instant before looking behind her for the gobbler. Despite your camouflage, you feel conspicuous. You try to pull together and wish it were possible to breathe with less movement. The hen scratches at the forest floor, then lifts her head and scrutinizes the ridge. Satisfied with the security, she lifts her wings in a stretching motion and fluffs up her feathers before taking two more steps.

The gobble hits you like a physical force. As soon as you hear the sound, you know what has happened. The gobble didn't come from the ridge, in the direction of the hen, but at a right angle and just off the contour. He has paralleled her approach just off the ridgetop. He is probably within thirty yards. If it were not for the hen, you could rotate ninety degrees and wait for him to pop up at the contour; however, the slightest movement will alert her, and that will be the end of the affair. You move your eyes to the edge of the ridge, feeling desperate. The hen comes closer. She is twenty-five yards away when she looks back down the ridge and makes a soft yelp. The gobble that greets her call is even closer. He has moved along the edge and is almost directly opposite you; despite being off the contour, he is probably closer than the hen. You swing your eyes to the left to focus on the spot from which the gobble came. Because it is a full ninety degrees to the left, your vision is blurred, and you consider slowly turning your head. Fifteen years of experience convinces you to reject the idea of movement.

The next sound is the puff of the strut. You can see the hen moving in front of you as you strain to focus on the ridge's drop-off. Your eyes water with the strain, and your vision blurs. You move your eyes back toward the hen. She is fifteen yards away. There is nothing you can do.

You see the dark blur at the edge of the drop-off and know instantly it is the top of his great tail, fanned out in his strut. He is climbing the ridge! Your breath comes quicker. The bird is fifteen yards away, but you are incapable of action. Your only chance is that he walk in front of you.

As you try to focus on the dark blur, the hen comes still closer. You glance back at her, and now she is not ten yards away. You will not go undetected much longer. A sudden flash of white tells you his head is now above the contour. You strain to see him clearly, but the rotation of your eyes continues to blur the image. His progress is slow but steady. The blurred shape grows, your pulse rate increases, and sweat runs down your face. The blur diminishes in size and you know he has gone out of strut. The sound waves of the incredibly loud gobble bounce off you. Your pulse can race no faster. The bird fluffs back into strut and moves slightly more into your line of vision. He is moving toward the hen and toward the aiming plane of your barrels. After several interminable seconds he comes into focus at an angle forty-five degrees from the direction in which your gun is pointed. He is twice the size of the hen. His massive beard hangs down, and despite the intensity of the moment, you notice that it is curved and bounces slightly with each step he takes. Just ten more yards and you can bring the gun on him.

Suddenly the hen putts. The gobbler freezes. The game is up—you have to act. You swing the gun. He does not flush. He does not run. He does the one thing that leaves you without a chance. He throws himself over the contour of the ridge in one violent motion and disappears. You jump up and stagger on cramped legs to the edge of the contour. You watch, helplessly, as he beats his way up above the trees eighty yards in front of you. The escape is perfect. He was fifteen yards away, and you were unable to get a shot.

You stand on the ridge and shake with the thrill. It is over; you will not get a second chance. Despite the disappointment, you are smiling. It has happened again. He was in the most precarious of positions and somehow extricated himself. You are proud of what he accomplished. No one could convince you that any other game could have exercised such a perfect escape.

-| -|

HOUDINI

My partner's first setter was not named Houdini, nor has Gary ever called him that. The dog was named Gable. The name is interesting. Gary is Washington and Lee University's wrestling coach. One of the great heroes of the fraternity of American college wrestlers is a gentleman named Dan Gable, who established remarkable winning records in high school, college and international competition. It is my understanding that many dogs, goldfish, and sons of wrestlers are named for the guy.

One day Gary took Gable to an area where he had seen turkey sign. Gary hoped to scatter birds so he and I could return to hunt the next morning. Being well prepared, he did carry a call and camouflage so he could set up to call the birds if he got into them early in the afternoon. If that occurred, his plan was to take the dog back to the car before trying to call. He did not hit the flock until three forty-five, and he was a good thirty-five-minute walk from his car. After building a blind, Gary decided to mark a trail to the somewhat isolated spot. He realized we could park closer to the flush area the next morning if we drove to another farm for access, so he began to mark that route. It was in the opposite direction of his car and, upon returning to the blind on his way back to the car, he realized it was only four o'clock and the woods were very quiet. Since he could get back to the car before dark if he left the blind by four thirty-five, and since he seemed to have forgotten, for a brief moment, that his partner was not with him, he decided to try to call a bird up *with* Gable.

You may wonder why he did not tie the setter to a tree a couple of hundred yards from the blind, but Gary had tried that twice before. The first time the dog got free just in time to flush a bird that was coming in. From that point forward, my name for the dog was Houdini. The second time the escape act failed, because Gary did a better job with his knots; however, Houdini still ruined the hunt. After several minutes the dog's barking changed to a muffled choking. Gary raced to him just in time to keep him from hanging himself. I told Gary that if he ever tied Houdini to a tree again, I would report him to the ASPCA.

So Gary had to try to keep the dog in the blind. He tried to hold him. The use of any mechanical call was out of the question, because Gary needed both hands for Houdini. My partner first tried his mouth call, which brought an immediate response from a young gobbler. Houdini heard the turkey and increased his struggling, so Gary had to use his legs as well as his arms to keep the big setter down. I would pay a hundred dollars to have the match on tape. I asked Gary if Houdini got any points for escapes or reversals—or got a handicap to make up for Gary's lifetime of on-the-job training in the wrestling room. Unfortunately, the rawboned setter was in much better shape than any of Gary's athletes. Even Gary admits the struggle was an epic event. Finally, he got his knees into the dog's chest cavity, and Houdini lost a bit of his enthusiasm. Directly on top of the dog now, Gary began to call more aggressively. He could hear the sounds of the approaching bird walking in the leaves. He could not let go of the dog to raise his gun, so he knew this would have to be a quick-draw effort. With his elbow, he moved the gun into position for a quick grab and began to look up the hill for the turkey. As he searched for the bird, he suddenly realized the dog was no longer struggling. He took a quick look down at Houdini and saw that his eyes had rolled up in his head, and his body was limp. The horrible had occurred: He had killed Houdini! He jerked his legs off the dog, loosened his grip on his neck, and whispered, "Gable, are you all right?" There was no response from the limp dog. Thanks to his CPR training, Gary knew what it would take to resuscitate the dog, and he began working frantically. Gary admitted that mouth-to-mouth resuscitation with a dog that samples every animal dropping in the woods is not pleasant. In fact, when he told the story in front of my wife and daughters, they left the room.

Meanwhile, the young gobbler was now disturbed that the turkey he had heard calling had stopped. He began to call with greater enthusiasm. Gable pulled another Houdini act by coming to life and, in typical dog fashion, wagged his tail at the master who had almost killed him.

The traumatic experience did make the dog reasonably docile, and Gary was able to turn his concentration from the dog he had almost killed to the turkey he wanted to kill. As luck would have it, it was only a couple of seconds after turning from the dog that Gary saw the young gobbler running down the slope toward him. Still afraid to let go of the dog, Gary waited until the bird was twenty yards away before he grabbed the gun and killed the bird. Wyatt Earp could have been no quicker. The released Houdini was on the fallen bird in a flash and began to maul it as poor Gary ran to save the mortally wounded turkey from the vindictive dog.

Candidly, I wrote this story about Houdini because I thought it was humorous; however, it offers a lesson for anyone thinking about training a dog to hunt wild turkeys. No matter how much experience you have had with dogs, the process of training one to be a finished turkey dog will be a immense challenge.

12

THE SELECTION OF THE TURKEY HUNTER

James is a turkey hunter. In his part of West Virginia, no sentence says more about a man. James is not a member of the NRA; he belongs to no hunt clubs; he subscribes to no outdoor journals; he does not hunt turkeys for human companionship. The aggressively masculine hunt camp is as uncomfortable to him as an urban bar.

James lives to hunt turkeys. His is the legacy of the hunter that historians say helped shape the nation's character and that anthropologists argue established the path of human evolution.

James has been captured, perhaps seduced, by the challenge that wild turkeys present and by the comfort he derives from those wild areas turkeys inhabit. James knows he is a good turkey hunter and he is proud of it. He takes satisfaction from the fact he is known as the best turkey hunter in Randolph County. He is neither a hermit nor a recluse. His tax statement says he is a forester. In fact, he is a turkey hunter who works as a forester because his culture does not subsidize hunting.

James lives for November and April, turkey seasons in his state. During November, his days average eighteen hours in length. He gets no overtime, and asks for none. He eats, sleeps, and hunts. On many occasions he sleeps and eats only enough to be able to hunt. In the spring turkeys begin to gobble at 4:30 A.M. To be in position at the top of a three-thousand-foot ridge, you have to wake at 2:30 A.M. I know, because I hunt with James. The season is thirty days long. He rarely misses a day. By the last day of the spring season he will look like one of Napoleon's defeated soldiers on the road back from Moscow. He will have hunted to the edge of exhaustion; occasionally, he falls over that edge.

He enjoys the fact that turkeys are tough, and appreciates the fact that "they make you bleed a little." Have you ever tried to climb up a mile-long, sixty-degree slope in seventy-degree April heat, bearing thirty pounds of clothes and equipment? Your legs cramp, your body aches, you wonder what the stress will do to your heart. You slip, the equipment pounds you onto the sharp limestone, and you grunt with very real pain. You get a sick feeling as you look up at the dark and distant ridge. Finally, you reach the ridge, find the tree, and sink onto the cool ground. You let your body collapse and you feel your heart struggle with the strain imposed by the climb. You look over the valley. You are proud of the perspective. You smile at James. He smiles back. This is essential human companionship: Two men attempting something difficult together; two friends who respect each other, celebrate each other's successes, and are sensitive to each other's failures.

The gobble makes the climb inconsequential. James is instantly alert. He registers the distance to the bird and plans the attack quickly. Gentle and soft spoken, James has now transformed into the most effective predator in the animal world. He runs toward the bird with agility and determination, his mind weighing all the necessary information. How far is the bird? How old? From where would it be best to call? Is he still on the roost? James's brain is his greatest asset.

James knows what it takes to kill turkeys regularly, and derives a sense of self-worth from his hunting success. Some call him lucky, but he knows better. His success and reputation are based exclusively on his competence. Dress, articulateness, wealth, education, status, or popularity mean nothing. His accomplishments are earned. Consistently taking wild turkeys is difficult. This is not killing a deer blinded by fear of an army of hunters. James knows that most men in hunt camps are not efficient hunters. He encounters them occasionally. They are either sitting in trees in silent ambush, incapable of more challenging hunting, or they barge through the woods riding on four-wheelers and carrying huge knives—obscene parodies of the efficient and proud human hunter.

Turkey hunting selects against the incompetent. True, the incompetent will enjoy occasional success, but they are not capable of consistent success under fair conditions. James avoids the incompetent in the woods. They are dangerous. I once sat with James and listened to a man call at my friend with a box call. The man was excited because he was sure James's call was a turkey. I thought it was funny. James wasn't amused, and told me, "That boy may fire a shot up here after a while. Then he'll go back to his camp and say he called one up close. They've shot at me a time or two. I wish these hills were even steeper so that we could get away from all of them, all of the time."

A day with James will provide a better testimony to the skill of human hunters than watching a movie of Bushmen killing a giraffe in the Kalahari Desert. Have you ever heard a really good turkey hunter run a call? James goes into himself. His blue eyes focus on something distant. No better testimony can be made to the skill of human hunters than the sound of a good one with a call.

James does not consider killing turkeys as secondary to some mystic experience in the woods. He loves to kill turkeys. He talks about the times he has called birds up and not killed them.

"I don't know why, but it's not the same. You remember when you took those photographs of the birds? It just wasn't the same. I like to be looking down the rib of the old Ithaca. I call better. You know I love my turkeys, and I pass up hens, but I enjoy killing them. It hasn't diminished at all. I still like to carry them out of the woods."

James is a wonderful woodsman, and when in the woods he is not oblivious to other creatures. I have watched him as he enjoyed the frolicking of young squirrels. He does not kill to answer some twisted need.

One summer evening, while riding up the mountain to search for young turkeys, we encountered a huge timber rattlesnake on the side of the road. James backed up to look at the snake, and the rattler came for the vehicle. James said, with obvious admiration and respect, "This truck is a thousand times bigger than he is, but that boy is standing his ground." It would have been easy to kill the snake, and it would have made the local newspaper. James never considered it.

James's turkey gun is a 10-gauge Ithaca double he bought at a hardware store in Elkins, West Virginia, in 1936. He has killed 119 turkeys with it. The gun fits the man. It is a credit to American ingenuity and craftsmanship. The gun is not as pretty as a Purdey, but this is an *American* gun. It was made for honest, decent men who were not born of noble lineage. When its price tag was a hundred dollars, the Purdey sold for two thousand. It is a testimony to the democratic nature of American hunting. The ten-and-a-half-pound gun is now a collector's item—and, like its owner, it is authentic. It is a reminder of a period when fine American shotguns were made by hand, by men who cared.

It's interesting that most of the great turkey hunters I know are armed with old Model 12 Winchesters, Browning automatics made in Belgium, L. C. Smiths, big Parkers, and Pre 1964 Model 70 Winchesters in .22 Hornet. These guns were made for people like James. The "semi-wild" preserves select for impressed checkering, plastic butt plates, stamped metal, and men who have been weaned on released birds and plastic guns.

The big Ithaca, carefully cleaned, hangs in James's modest home. In other sections of this country fine guns hang waiting to be used by capable men. Their hunting knowledge and competence will match that of any German in the Black Forest or Scot on the Isle of Skye. They provide proof that contemporary hunting selects for competent, tough, skilled, and intelligent humans and affords them enjoyment, satisfaction, fulfillment, and pride.

13

THE FIRST DAY

I hit the door hard as I rush to leave the building. My body is tight with anticipation, and I smile at my eagerness. Tomorrow is the first day and I am free to hunt for a week.

It is cool in the quiet town as I park the vehicle in front of the small hardware store. The "hunting display" is in the window, as it is every November. It is always the same: a moth-eaten turkey gobbler, poorly mounted years ago, standing in an unnatural pose above an assortment of cheap hunting accessories.

The shop is warm and friendly, and I move through the cramped aisles with ease. Ostensibly, the purpose of my visit is to purchase shotgun shells; however, I still have an adequate supply from the year before. I am really here because it is the day before turkey season opens. The relaxed moments in the familiar shop provide a symbolic prelude to the long-awaited day. A clerk, and friend, greets me and asks if he can be of help. I point to a specific box of shells from the many on the shelves and help him locate them by saying, "The Federal, three-inch, one and five-eighths ounce, Number 6 shot." Junior picks up the box, hands it to me, touches me on the shoulder, and asks, "How many turkeys are in that box, John?" The question is a compliment and I appreciate it. I mutter something about how I hope there is *one,* in a weak attempt at modesty.

There are several prospective turkey hunters in the store. One middle-age man stands in front of a mirror and tries on a camouflage hat. The hat is enough to make anyone look foolish, but when it is balanced on top of a bright blue leisure suit, which is stretched to accommodate a broad girth, the effect is incredible. To the left of the fat man a large high school student stands gazing at a turkey call that rests in his powerful hand. Another salesman stands in front of the boy. He, too, is looking at the call. The boy doesn't know enough to ask an intelligent question. Finally he says, "This is the best one, right?" The salesman ducks the question by saying, "We sell a whole lot of those calls." The boy continues to stare at the object in his hand, and then reaches for his billfold.

Another older man holds a new shotgun in his hand as he talks to the store manager. The man's wife looks on from several aisles away. Her distance is testimony to the difficulty women have in entering the subculture of hunting in small southern towns. The woman looks on the masculine domain with self-conscious impatience. The husband ignores his wife as he continues to ask inane questions about the gun. He points it at an imaginary target for the tenth time and says, "This will kill one as far as any shotgun, right?" The manager says, "Yes, it should." The manager's tone is low, and he appears to be embarrassed. The customer turns to his wife and says with greater assurance, "This will kill us a whole lot of turkeys." His wife's only response is to raise her eyes to meet his. There is no support of his statement, just a cold stare. The manager turns away from the potential domestic confrontation to place another gun in the rack.

Robert, a turkey hunter, has just entered the store. His eyes catch mine and he smiles. He is not here to look at guns or calls.

He knows it is too late for that. He is here to share the excitement with others who see the next day as being as important as he does. I enjoy his company. We come from diverse backgrounds, and our occupations are as different as any can be. With the exception of wild turkeys, we share little in common. But the bond created by a passion for hunting turkeys is enough. The odd connection makes me feel closer to him than the people with whom I work. We talk briefly about the status of the turkey population. His eyes sparkle with anticipation. After a short conversation, we wish each other luck and I walk to the front of the store to pay for the shells.

"Welcome home, turkey hunter," Nell says as I walk out of the dark November evening into the bright house. "Oh my goodness, a new box of shells, those poor turkeys." I smile at the teasing. I have had the incredible good fortune to share a life with a woman who respects my passion for hunting. She takes the opportunity to tease me when I go over the edge in my obsessiveness, but she takes pride in my skill and the commitment I have to the birds; she enjoys the immense satisfaction I derive from them. She has communicated this respect to our daughters.

The girls tease me about my preoccupation during dinner, and when the phone rings, Catherine, who is only seven, says, "I bet it is Gary and he wants to talk to his playmate." Nell and our older daughter, Elizabeth, laugh louder than necessary to celebrate Cath's well-timed tease. It *is* my hunting partner and I seek refuge from the now-aggressive teasing to make plans for the first day. The conversation is filled with landmarks we have established on our favorite property over the years. "We can cover it better if I go in from the camp and you enter from McCabe's," says Gary. "That way I can cover the High Field and Reed's Ridge and you can hit Photographic Knoll, McCabe's Main Ridge, and the Pond Hollow. We can meet at Bussard's Saddle if we don't get into them." None of the names are on any published maps. The rest of the conversation turns to considerations of time and reports from other hunters.

I look at my watch and realize there is a lot to accomplish before retiring. I go to the basement and begin to get my gear together. As I spread the equipment around the room, my mind drifts to other first days. Each piece of equipment brings back memories. I've carried a few items since I was a boy, and I feel a strong sentimental attachment to them. There is a wonderful excitement but also a bit of tension as I try to make my deadline for bed. Suddenly I wonder about the gas in my vehicle, and I panic and rush upstairs and out to the car. Nell hears the speed of my departure and asks if everything is okay. Over my shoulder, I call out and tell her I forgot to check the fuel in the car. It is low, and I return to the house to tell Nell I have to go out. As I ride through town, I feel the tension of making my bedtime deadline and am mad at myself for not having checked the gas. When I return home, Nell is aware of my anxiety and says, "I'll set the tea up for tomorrow." She knows that will save me some time. I thank her and return to check everything in the basement. A successful inventory of the gear provides reassurance.

It is hard to relax, and sleep does not come easy as the excitement runs through me. At some stage in my anticipation, I fall asleep.

As always on the first day, I awake before the alarm. Later in the enervating season, I will be embarrassed when Nell will have to tell me the alarm is going off, but now I am rested. I move carefully to avoid disturbing her. I enjoy the predawn hours, when the house and town are insulated from twentieth-century noises. I eat my light breakfast quickly and hurry to the car. I am ahead of my self-imposed schedule, and feel both comfortable and eager as I ride through the deserted town and into the hills. I go over the hunt I have planned in my mind. The fact that it is the first day makes it particularly exciting. One highly relevant factor is that I am rested; my mind, as well as my muscles, benefits from the strength I feel. My optimism is fueled by the fact I have a whole season stretching before me.

I pass a gas station, and the cars crowded in front of the store are full of guys in camouflage. At this stage, all are optimistic. I do not stop, as many would, because I do not enjoy the crowds. The solitary nature of turkey hunting probably selects for nongregarious personality types. I celebrate the enjoyment those at the store are deriving from the communal start, but it is not for me.

I smile as I remember my early first days. Those were always on the last Saturday in October, and the game that made the day the most important of the year for me was the pheasant. My mother would often take her too-eager young son to farms where good friends had given us permission to hunt. I remember the exciting rides vividly. I was always worried that there would be men who would beat me to the best spots. The most intense emotion during the rides was anxiety. From my earliest days, the *success* of the first day was important. I did not hunt to have fun: I hunted to kill pheasants. As a boy, I worked at it. That has not changed.

On this day I was confident I would be free from competition. The difference was the size of the area to be hunted. The cornfields of Bucks County were small, and the numbers of pheasant hunters immense. Here in western Virginia the woods are large and the numbers of hunters far fewer than those generated by the large cities that were close to Bucks County's wonderful fields. I smiled at the memories of the other first days.

It was a quick trip, and I soon saw the familiar entrance and pulled onto the gravel road. A short time later I parked where I always stop, and rushed to get into the mountains. There was no need to hurry, but something pressed me to get to my spot—the same way, as a kid, I was always at the edge of the corn *first*. It was the First Day and I wanted to capture every possible second. As I began to walk toward the dark trees beyond the field, I looked up at the ridges to see if there were any flashlights. I saw none. I picked up the pace and felt myself begin to breathe deeply as both the climb and the excitement began to impact my body. I knew I was not the only guy thrilled to be charging into the darkness.

14

THE TOUGHEST GAME IN TOWN

As is usually the case with fall gobblers, this was an unusual hunt. Because it was exam week at the university, I had the opportunity to hunt for two full days, and decided to follow up on a tip I had received from one of the area's best deer hunters. He told me about a gang of mature gobblers he had seen in an isolated section of the county. My plan was to invest two days in trying to find them.

At dawn on the first of my precious days, I was high on Short Hill Mountain with my Chesapeake bitch, Sage. We were close to the spot where my friend had seen the turkeys. We did not hear a sound. I made a couple of blind calls and hoped my lack of confidence was not obvious in my calling. There was no answer.

At eight-thirty we began the tough search. There would be no shortcuts. As stiff and cold as we were, it was nice to begin walking. I thought about where to search, but there were no easy answers. The area was vast and we could only cover a small part of it no matter how great our effort. We found old sign, but by noon we had not seen a bird. It was gratifying to see that Sage was also tired. I sat back against a large white oak to let my body rest, and I shared my meager lunch with her. I enjoyed Sage's company.

I love the big hardwoods that are part of the turkey hunter's domain. I knew I would remember this tree in the future and watch it grow. I hate to see them cut or blown down. They become more than landmarks. I once told a friend I was going to photograph the largest oaks I have found in Rockbridge County. He asked, "Why?" I heard myself say, "Because I love them."

It was tempting to stay at the oak and try some calls, but I knew that to have any chance of success we had to find the flock. After the rest, I felt stronger and decided to try a high basin in which I had once found the largest morel mushrooms I have ever seen.

We flushed a pair of grouse from a deadfall as we entered the highest bench in the hollow. I will always remember where that deadfall is. I may forget names, but twenty years in the future, if my body is able, I will be able to take you to the deadfall. For me, remembering where I find game is so important that I consider it atavistic.

We were high on the mountain when the Chesapeake hit the scent. She got very excited before striking up the steep side of the hollow. I followed as rapidly as I could. I knew I had to get to the ridgetop a short time after Sage to have a chance to see the birds. My heart was pounding, and wondered how smart it was imposing such stress on my fifty-year-old body. The thought did not alter my pace. A scant five yards from the top I heard the Chessie bark and I knew she was into them. I felt the adrenaline make me pull even harder. I looked up as I gained the ridgetop and saw two birds sail down the hollow and two more run up the opposing ridge. I watched, hoping other birds would flush, but saw no more; still, "we" had scattered the flock.

It was twelve thirty-five, ample time for the birds to try to get back together before dark. It was not long before the dog returned. She was panting hard and I took her down into the hollow, where she had a long drink and then lay down in the stream. I hoped we would capitalize on her great effort. After a good rest, we headed up the slope to find a spot to build a blind. The ridge was wide, and there were many mature hardwoods. I selected a beautiful chestnut oak in the middle of the ridge and began to construct my blind. It did not take long. When I finished, I arranged my gear in the small space and coaxed the dog in to join me. It was wonderful to rest. I was still warm from the exertion, and I felt comfortable. I looked forward to the afternoon. It was one twenty-five. I decided not to call until I heard one of the mature birds. If I did not hear a call by four o'clock, I would make a single series of yelps. Sage had trouble understanding the strategy of waiting, and pawed at me in boredom.

The cold began to attack us. I zipped up my jacket and pulled my body together. Sage coiled up in the blind. It was going to be a cold afternoon.

The time went rapidly. I watched a squirrel for a while and then listened to the progress of a grouse hunt far below us in the rough cover at the base of the mountain. I heard several shotgun shots and the clear whistle of a hunter. I love to hunt grouse, but I was pleased to be high on the mountain after turkeys. I am unashamedly proud of the fact that so few hunters try for mature gobblers in the fall. Those of us who do are part of a special group. It is far and away the toughest game in town.

At three-thirty I began to strain for the sound of a call. A single cluck is not loud, and it is easy to miss if you are not attentive—and particularly if a lifetime with shotguns has taken a toll on your hearing. I heard nothing.

"Have they gotten together at another location? Will they stay separated for several days? Have they been fooled with before?" My mind flirted with the possibilities, and the falling light and increasing cold contributed to my anxiety. Sage was sick of my passive strategy. Understandably impatient, she tried to whine until I put her ear in my mouth and bit it. She yelped and looked at me with clear contempt, but she did not whine. I smiled to myself, aware that there are only five people in the world she would allow to bite her ear; four are members of my nuclear family, and the fifth is my hunting partner.

At four-fifteen I decided to make the fateful calls. I am always intimidated when I call to old gobblers in the fall, because I really don't want to make a mistake. I took out the special wing-bone made by my good friend Rich Tiberio. This call has revolutionized my fall hunts. The loud yelps sounded good. I waited for a response. There was none.

I decided to wait until absolute darkness before leaving the blind. No turkey would come to me after flying-up time, but if one *had* heard my call, I wanted to be sure he did not identify me as I left the woods. A lot of hunters do not like darkness, but I enjoy the isolation it provides. The walk out of the woods warmed my body. I felt good when we got to the vehicle.

I saw Nell look out at the car as I pulled into the driveway. I felt guilty because I recognized she must always feel fear when I am out there alone, late, with a firearm. I gave Sage extra food and tried to make it up to the dogs I had not taken. I enjoyed the sounds of my family as I entered the warm house.

When Gary answered the phone I explained what had occurred. I began to tell him that I thought we had a chance when he cut me off and said, "Sorry, Doc, I promised Linda and the kids we would go to Roanoke tomorrow; you'll be on your own."

It is hard to sit in a blind all day and suffer in the cold with the clear knowledge that the birds will probably not come. If Gary had been able to join me, it would have been easier. The news that I would be alone made me begin to search for an excuse not to go. I would enjoy going after young birds with the dog, but with old gobblers I was afraid to take the dog: Despite her discipline, she might sneeze or shake her head or make some tiny movement that the birds would detect. I could grade exams tomorrow morning, or—a more attractive idea—see if the black ducks were on the river, or. . . .

It is very different in the spring. There is never a moment when I don't have confidence I can call in a bird. With good calling, spring birds will come at any time. In the fall the time I invest is often futile if they have gotten back together, or if they are going to wait another day, or if they are going to get together somewhere else. So I found myself trying to find an excuse for not punishing my body. My younger daughter came up behind me and said, "Are you going after them, Dad?" I answered, "I am not sure, Cath; I have a lot to do." She responded with a quick, "Go for it!" It struck a chord. I smiled at her and walked out into the cold evening. The sky was bright and I felt the adrenaline begin to pump as my mind reflected on the distant ridge and the big *mature* birds.

The next morning I was at the base of the mountain. It would take me almost an hour of steady climbing to get to where they had flushed. The distant ridge, visible in the moonlight, seemed impossibly far away. I turned away from the mountain, put the pack on, picked up my gun, and started off.

The first hundred yards were tough. I had to climb over a fence and felt awkward. My body and legs were stiff; there was some pain in my lower back where I had recently had surgery. But I soon fell into a pace, my body began to warm up, and I knew I would be fine. The rest of the trip was a persistent climb. I stopped twice and, as always, was surprised by how hot I was despite the cold. Years of climbing with firearms have taught me how to shift the Benelli from one arm to another to keep it from feeling heavy. My steady gait ate up the terrain. I began to enjoy being on the mountain. I thought about my strategy as I walked. With young birds it is all relatively easy; any call will work. Now I agonized over which call to use. It did not help that in the past I have had many more failures than successes.

When I found the blind I opened my jacket, sat down, and waited for dawn. At first light I would make one wildcat call—a long, whistle made by a lost old gobbler. It is rarely imitated. After the one wildcat call, I would make no other calls until fifteen minutes after flying-down time, when I would yelp once. I would wait a full hour to make another call.

It was a typical late-December morning. The woods seemed deserted, and I was sure there were few hunters afield; most had used up their free days in pursuit of deer. I grew impatient waiting to call, but I knew if I did so too soon I would have no chance of success. Finally the time passed and I prepared to make the yelps. A considerable measure of insecurity gripped me as I realized I would probably be frustrated once again. There here have been years in which I have not called in a single old boy in the fall.

After making the call, I felt a tightness in my body. I held my breath as I strained for a response. The anticipation dissipated. My anxiety turned to frustration. My mind turned to the black ducks that I was sure were on the river. I thought, "I will try that tomorrow with Sage and. . . ."

A coarse yelp from down the mountain cut off my daydream. It could have been another hunter, but I knew it was not. My heart began to race. I was sure he expected me to call back, and my fear of not making a good call was immense. This was not just another morning in the spring. With old gobblers in the fall, every chance is treasured—it may be the only one in two years. I had to build up my confidence before I was ready to kiss the wingbone. Finally I did, and was pleased with the tone. Even if he did not respond, I knew my call was good.

I let the wingbone hang down naturally on its lanyard, checked my facemask, and moved slightly to face the direction from which I had heard the call. I did not expect a response. I tried to relax and told myself to be calm. The pep talk was futile. When a small branch dropped out of a nearby tree, I felt my body jerk with the tension that held me. My right leg was cramped, but I was afraid to move. This was no time to worry about comfort. I crouched lower in the blind, trying to make myself invisible. I strained to hear the sound of footsteps. My eyes blurred with the cold. I blinked quickly with the childish notion that the bird could appear as I was blinking. My anticipation turned to anxiety as ten minutes became fifteen.

"You screwed it up again; you should not have made another call," I said to myself. I felt myself sigh with the sense of failure. Then, not a second later, I heard the footsteps. There was no question it was a turkey: The gait and pace were perfect. He was coming right up the ridge. I moved slightly and looked down the rib of my gun. My heart began to pound. The footsteps stopped, and I held my breath. Experience told me he was probably still sixty yards away, but I knew how wary he was. When the footsteps began again, I heard myself exhale. The steady crunching of the leaves on the frozen forest floor was loud, and my tension increased even more. He stopped again. The tension was enough to produce pain. The muscles of my shoulders and neck burned; I strained to maintain composure. Waiting for him to move, I realized I could not maintain my position much longer. I had my gun braced on the blind, but my arms were beginning to tremble. When the footsteps began again, they seemed too loud. I wondered if my less-than-perfect hearing was playing tricks on me, and I resisted the temptation to look down the ridge. The sudden flash of movement was just to the left of where my gun barrel pointed, and I made the tiny adjustment with my hands as the bird appeared some forty-five yards away. Instantly, the big red head jerked upright. I shot by instinct and with neither composure nor confidence. The shooting computer in my brain, programed by years of experience, took over. I could not tell you exactly where I held on the bird. I knew I had no time to spare.

I tried to stand, but my cramped right leg failed and I fell flat. On essentially one leg, I scrambled to where the bird had been. There was no turkey. I looked down the steep slope on the edge of the ridge and saw a trail of feathers. Experience told me that if I had missed, he would have flushed, but I was still too insecure to accept that he had rolled down the hill with his head and neck riddled with shot. I would have felt differently if he were a young bird, but he wasn't. The possibility of not finding him sent me down the slope in reckless pursuit. I careered down the grade on my one good leg, oblivious to the danger of a bad fall. I saw flecks of blood with the feathers, and it was bright. The blood lifted my spirits. I reached out to a small hardwood, spun around with the momentum of my descent, and saw him immobile against a dead-fall. He was huge and beautiful. The range of colors in his feathers was breathtaking. With his massive head and power-ful legs, he looked bigger then they do in spring—and, to me, he was. I threw my right arm up in the air and yelled, "Yes!" The sheer thrill of it ran through me. I used to yell like that when I killed a spring gobbler and, years ago, with deer. Now such unrestrained celebration is reserved exclusively for ma-ture fall gobblers. It is not heard often.

15

TURKEY-HUNTING FATIGUE

Turkey hunting is exhausting. The fatigue is a function of the physical demands and the duration of the hunts. I have the luxury of living less than half an hour from many superb hunting properties, but in spring I still set my alarm for 3:30 A.M. Nothing will keep a string of 3:30 A.M. starts from draining you. You can try to get to bed early, or you can sneak a nap, but you will not escape the fatigue.

It does not help that the best areas for turkey hunting afford very little easy walking. The terrain is rarely flat or open. Swamps and hardwood ridges afford much more difficult walking than corn- or broom sage fields.

Most of us carry a lot of gear while turkey hunting. When I returned from one particularly enervating fall hunt, I decided to weigh all the gear and clothes I had carried or worn. The weight was a shocking forty-three pounds. When I assessed each item, I didn't find anything I could discard.

Try carrying forty-three pounds of gear up and down Appalachian slopes. That represents 27 percent of my body weight. You can go to the best gym in the country, but you still won't get a workout that comes close to climbing steep ridges with forty-three pounds of gear.

THE IMPACT OF TURKEY-HUNTING FATIGUE

One of your first clues that you are *too* tired is losing things. One index I have learned to use is how often I forget where I have placed my shooting glasses. By the time I get to the spot from which I will begin my hunt, my glasses are invariably fogged up with body heat. How well I remember where I put the glasses is a function of my level of fatigue. Early in the season, I never forget. As the fatigue wears me down, I have trouble finding them.

One of the more humorous experiences my partner and I had with fatigue in spring involves the use of the telephone. It is rare that we miss communicating with each other in the evening. One spring my partner got so tired he would dial my home number when he intended to call his family. The story is true. My daughters would pick up the phone only to realize that poor, exhausted Gary had unconsciously dialed our number once again.

The fatigue can have more dramatic impacts on the hunter.

STORY 1—THE SPRING ASSAULT

Early in our careers Gary and I were hunting together during the last week of the spring season. We were so tired that we didn't have the strength to talk as we ate breakfast. On this particular morning we had to open several gates to reach our hunting area. At the first gate, my partner got out and opened it as I drove through. As I waited for him to return to the vehicle, I felt the numbness in my body from the fatigue. I was reflecting on how tired I was when I realized my partner had opened the driver's door and, with a glazed look in his eyes, was trying to climb into my seat. The most incredible thing about the entire experience was how slow I was to pick up on the bizarre error. It was not until Gary had all but grabbed the steering wheel that we recognized what had happened. While the story has elicited laughter from our friends, it demonstrates how irrational you can become from intense fatigue. It is not safe to be *that* tired.

STORY 2—NUMB

This story concerns a good friend who worked the 3-to-11 P.M. shift at a chemical plant. Every night he would make a tough one-hour drive home and get to bed just after midnight. When you retire at midnight, three-thirty comes very quickly. My friend found the courage—and I choose that word with care—to get out of bed at 3:30 A.M. *every day* of the season. Put in a week of 3:30 A.M. mornings, even when you are getting to bed at 9 P.M. rather than midnight, and you'll appreciate the toughness of that schedule.

My friend was okay for the first two weeks of the season. True, he had his moments. He got tired of his coworkers sneaking up behind him to gobble in his ear as he drifted to sleep on the job, and his drive home at eleven at night was torture. By the third week he was in pain, but he still was going hard.

It happened the next-to-last Saturday. He awoke, and both of his feet felt as if they were asleep. He told me that he thought he had just "lain down the wrong way or something." As he drove out to hunt, though, the numbness in his feet remained. Suddenly he realized his hands were kind of numb, too. "My God," he thought, "I'm going numb."

And the sensation would not go away. Days later, his coworkers were sure he was over the edge when he began to stomp his feet and shake his hands on the job. "It was terrible, John," he told me. "At times the feeling would come back, but most of the time my hands and feet were totally numb."

Numb's wife, Louise Virginia, even called my wife Nell to ask if I could prevail upon him to get some rest. She told Nell that their daughter kept asking, "Why does Daddy keep stomping his feet?" Once Louise Virginia went to the kitchen for a moment during dinner and suddenly heard her daughter say, "That's not nice, Daddy." When she returned to the dining room, Numb was asleep with his face in the mashed potatoes.

The worst incident occurred the last week of the season. Numb had located a huge gobbler and had gotten close two mornings in a row. Numb or not, there was no thought of rest. "You know how it is, John; he had one of those *superthick* beards!" By this time his general fatigue had become progressively worse. In his words:

> I'd sit up against a tree and couldn't keep my eyes open. The only thing that would keep me awake was his gobble. It got so bad the last Friday, that I was fighting sleep as he came toward me. I'd make a call, he'd double-gobble back, and an instant later I'd feel my eyes start to drop. I kept calling so his gobble would keep me awake. When he got about seventy-five yards away, I tried to lift the gun and I couldn't feel it. I jammed my hands into the ground a few times and got a little feeling back in my fingers. I didn't dare move my legs because I couldn't feel my feet. That bird came on toward me, and for the first time I didn't shake. God, it was nice not to be trembling and panting! Well, I finally got my gun up, and at the shot he just flopped on the ground. Instead of jumping up, I just sat there sort of stunned. I mean, I was so numb I couldn't move. It took me several minutes to get up. When I was finally up, I realized I hadn't picked up my slate call, and when I leaned down for it, I fell over! It was terrible. I must have looked like an old turtle rolling around. Finally, I got up and staggered over to the bird, and I started stomping to try to get the circulation back. It must have been a sight, John. There I am, standing over this great gobbler, stamping my feel and shaking my hands. I mean, most of me was numb!

My friend has carried the nickname *Numb* ever since that year. I wish I had taken Numb to a physician to get a clinical assessment. I'm sure his fatigue had reached such a point that a diagnosis could have been made about what physiologically was taking place. I am happy to report that two weeks after the season concluded, the numbness disappeared and my friend's health returned.

It is my hope that both of these stories were amusing. However, it is also important for all of us to be aware of just how dangerous fatigue can be. If two men of average intelligence can climb on top of one another in a car, is it not possible for them to do things that are dangerous? I have to answer with an emphatic *yes*. Be aware of how fatigue can impact you!

·] 6

ESCAPE

It is easy to forget what a gift it is to be hunting when all is well. I learned that grim lesson in the spring of 1980 when my father was dying of cancer. The disease was diagnosed in August 1979, and he declined rapidly. By that spring he was in excruciating pain. Each day I called my mother to ask, "How is he?" She would say, "Fair." *Fair* could be translated as "terrible." When I saw him, I agonized over his physical deterioration—and marveled at his spirit.

The week before the season began I walked into his room and asked how he was. He somehow fought off the pain, toxins, and medication enough to say evenly, "It is a terrible disease." The comment was objective, as if offered by a student of the pathology rather than by a victim. As I looked at him, unable to respond, he pulled his failing strength together, smiled at me, and said simply, "I am not afraid." Suddenly, my three-year-old daughter ran into the room, screamed, "Mac!" and jumped onto the edge of the bed. His smile was the kind only Liz could generate.

As I drove home with my daughter, I looked at the fading light and wondered if I might have time to hear one gobble. When I walked into the kitchen, I told Nell I needed to get out and might be late for dinner. She said, "Just go; dinner can wait."

As I started up the familiar trail, the sounds and smells of the mountain seemed more powerful than normal. I felt the strength of my body as I climbed. The woods were comforting, and while I did not hear a gobbler, I returned home with renewed courage.

The first Monday of the season my father had an appointment with a physician in Charlottesville. When I picked him up, he was so thin it took my breath away. His spirit was intact, though, and he tried to make me laugh about his "weight loss" as we struggled to the car. Ten miles out of town he began to reel from the pain. He said we had to stop, and I pulled into a service station and watched, helplessly, as he stretched his back to try to reduce the pain. I have passed that same gas station hundreds of times since, and each time I think about the terrible trip in May 1980.

There was the inevitable but excruciating waiting at the clinic. I felt myself pull together against the chemical smells. Finally the young physician came in, greeted my father, and said effusively, "Haven't we done well since August!" After a moment of confusion, I recognized that he was celebrating the fact my dying father was still alive. I watched the terrible examination and felt as if the physician's hands were violating my own body rather than what was left of my father's. In the middle of the exam a nurse opened the door and said, "Excuse me, gentlemen. Doctor, you have an important call." I heard the physician say something about a tee time and then he moved out of the room, laughing. My father began to cry. After several seconds, he composed himself and said, "Don't tell your mother I cried." I don't remember how we got out of the clinic and back to Lexington.

My father was too tired and in too much pain to talk when I helped my mother and the nurse take him to his bed. I should have stayed to comfort my mother, but I didn't. When I pulled out of the driveway for the short trip home, the mountain entered my mind. I stopped at home only for a hectic moment as I raced to the basement to grab my boots and belt pack. The girls were out, and I left a barely legible note that read, "Need to get out—on Green Mountain—*high*—Gary will know where—may be back after dark. Love, Me."

I drove by instinct as my mind reflected on the horrors of the day. The turn off the main road came as a surprise, and I was frightened by my preoccupation. Still, I felt a renewed excitement in getting away. The emotion grew as I pushed through the thick grouse cover at the base of the mountain and headed for the hardwoods. I went up the first slope at a run. Gasping for air, I felt pain in my chest and legs. I saw fresh sign in the leaves and picked up my pace. When I reached my spot, my pulse raced and sweat ran down my face.

When the gobble came it was loud, healthy, and defiant. I knew where he was but I wanted to hear the sound again, so I hooted like an owl. The gobbler responded, instantly. I realized I was smiling. I was sure he was on the next spur ridge and that he would be there in the morning. I waited until it was fully dark; I did not want to risk him seeing me when I climbed off the ridge. The warm spring day cooled quickly and I listened to the sounds of the evening in the big woods. As the thermal air currents began to descend, I smelled the rich odors of spring and felt myself relax.

Soon the sun was down and I began to enjoy the sounds and smells of the night. I stayed longer than necessary and then began the dark descent off the mountain. Excited about the developments of the evening, I tried to jump across the creek and fell, hitting my lower leg on a rock. I saw the jagged gash that the blood had not yet found. I watched in fascination rather than fear as the bright blood ran down my leg, which looked too white in the darkness. Playing Boy Scout, I pulled off my old camouflage shirt and tried to tear a strip of it to wrap the wound. Unfortunately, the shirt did not tear, and I twisted it in a parody of the competent Eagle Scout. I reached for my wallet, in which I carried a tiny knife. I cut the shirt and made a rough bandage.

The first aid would not have earned me a merit badge, but it stopped the bleeding.

I was a different person as I got into the vehicle I had left ninety minutes before. The pain in my lower leg was no problem. I knew it would not keep me from returning the next morning. My thoughts on the ride to town were about the great bird. I could feel the transformation in my being. I was soaked with sweat, dirty, and my warm, sticky blood soaked rapidly through the ugly bandage—but the mountain had restored my spirit.

I called my mother after dinner and asked about my father. Her voice told me their afternoon had been as bad as mine had been good. I felt no guilt. I wished I could lift it from her but I knew that she would celebrate my evening success. "Tell him I am going after one in the morning." I was not at all sure my father would understand the message, but I knew he would be excited for me if he could.

It was easy to get up the next morning. I felt strong. The pain in my leg was dull and the cut looked clean. Soon I was in the vehicle and headed toward the mountain.

The climb was not the reckless event of the previous evening. I took my time and moved with care. I was pleased to see no evidence of other hunters. As usual, I found the tree more easily than I had anticipated.

I could not resist making a few soft tree calls on the Chisholm at first light. There was no response, but I hadn't expected any. I was sure the gobbler had heard the calls. His first gobble was well after first light. He was precisely where he had been the evening before. I would wait several minutes and then make some light clucks and purrs.

When I made the calls he gobbled furiously. I loved it and felt myself smile. The next sounds I heard were not so enjoyable: the loud cutting of a hen some one hundred yards down the mountain. As I was trying to determine the precise location of the turkey, another hen began to yelp even farther down the ridge. It was discouraging to listen to the gobbler go crazy in response to each of the awakening hens. I realized I had been naive to think that I could compete with his large harem.

I decided to move down the mountain toward the hens. My descent was all but reckless as I tried to get close to the hens before the gobbler did. I was racing down the side of a small spur ridge, using the ridgetop to conceal both me and the noise I was making. I enjoyed the wild sprint. There was the very real risk of a bad fall, but it added to the thrill. When I felt I was on the same level as the hens, I stopped and eased to the ridgetop to see where they were. I heard their still-loud calling from several points on the adjacent ridge. I wondered whether I could get to their ridge before the gobbler flew to them. I moved quickly down the slope, my entire being focused.

My involvement with the birds had provided a complete insulation from the horror of my father's situation. It was the *consuming* commitment to the hunt that was critical. If I had gone to watch a ballgame, the pace of the spectator sport would have allowed my mind to drift back to my father. Here on this remote mountain, I was totally absorbed.

I flushed one hen when I reached the other ridge, but the rest continued to call. I selected a large oak and sat up against it as I tried to get my breath. I was gasping from the strain of the climb as I reached into the belt pack for my calls. I looked up the mountain. He had gobbled several times as I sat, but it was his next call that allowed me to assess with some confidence where he was. "Not much over a hundred yards," I thought, and realized I had been lucky not to flush him. I made several loud yelps on the call and was quickly answered by a hen. The calling was great, as the turkeys made the mountain ring with their collective excitement. I paused in my calling, mostly in the interest of resting, when the sound of the gobbling changed and it grew clear that the bird was on the ground. He sounded farther away, but I knew it was simply because the sound waves were being interrupted by the vegetation between us. I could hear several hens yelping as they moved toward the area from which the gobbles had come. Once he collected his girls, I knew he would gobble at me but not come. After several moments it sounded as if all the birds were together and moving up the ridge.

My mind went over the topography of the mountain: The ridge intersected with a large bench some two hundred yards above where the birds were. East of this intersection was open hardwoods; west was a dense thicket of greenbrier. My bet was that the birds would move into the open hardwoods. To avoid detection, I would have to ambush them via a long, circuitous route. It would be a tough climb. I took a couple of seconds to make sure I had all my gear together, then set off at a run. Ten minutes into the move my breath was coming in gasps. After twenty minutes I reached the bench. Now the mad rush was transformed into a stalk as, gasping, I tiptoed onto the flat.

When I reached a large oak, I stopped and listened. The silence was not encouraging. I sat and went through the ritual of preparing to be there for a while. It was a beautiful flat. These benches are often found near the top of our mountains, and some of our most beautiful trees grow on them. In addition to the large oaks, there was an impressive collection of beech trees. The flat gray bark of the beeches was not scarred by any of the penknife marks so often cut into them by inconsiderate hikers and hunters in more accessible regions. I was enjoying the trees when the sound waves of the gobble hit me. My hearing was not good enough to give me a fix on one gobble, but my sense was that he was only a hundred yards away. At least I had guessed correctly about the route they would take.

The prudent strategy would have been to wait to see if he and his hens might just walk up to me—but I have never liked to play a passive role with gobblers. I couldn't resist the temptation to call. I make a quick, soft yelp on the Chisholm, and I was rewarded with an aggressive gobble. Now I would wait. I had my gun up and was beginning to breathe in a reasonable manner. Things looked good. Ten minutes passed without a sound. I tried another call. No answer. Five minutes later I tried a D. D. Adams glass call. Nothing. After another *long* ten minutes, I decided to try the louder Morgan tube call. After my first yelps I was rewarded with the quick, almost angry, cutting of a hen. I quickly called back at the bird, and she answered. I imitated her calls; again she responded. Soon another hen yelped loudly, and I thought I might be able to bring the hens to me. If they came, their macho friend might follow.

The hens *were* coming closer. They were so close that I put the Morgan down, let the diaphragm I had between my cheek and teeth slip into position on my palate, and looked down the rib of my shotgun.

The trim hen stepped boldly from behind a big beech. I love watching them call. Her head bobbed with the coarse yelps. I clucked back, and the small head turned toward me. She was forty-five yards away. I looked behind her and saw movement as another hen appeared, and then another. My eyes ignored each beautiful bird as I tried to penetrate the cover behind them to find the gobbler.

The first thing I saw was the fan of his tail. I moved slightly to bring my gun to bear. Hens were around him, and I cautioned myself to make sure they were not in the line of fire when his head came clear. The tail folded and the immense head and neck came into view. He was a long way out for the shotgun—at least forty-five yards. I felt my finger move to the second trigger on the big double to select the BBs. I told myself to hold at the base of his neck and moved the gun slightly until the white bead was superimposed on his bronze chest.

After the shock of the recoil, the scene was pandemonium. Flushing turkeys filled my field of view. I staggered to my feet and ran toward where the bird had been. Halfway to the spot my eyes were drawn to movement. I saw his huge head sticking up from the ground cover. The large shot had immobilized him. I moved closer and sensed that the bird was incapable of running or flying. When I approached he did not try to hide; nor did he show fear. His eyes were defiant. As a kid, I had seen the same courage in the eyes of pheasants. I grabbed his powerful neck and snapped it with as quick a motion as the strength in my arm allowed. I sat next to him and let the calmness come.

The trip back to town was peaceful. My mind turned to my father, and I hoped he would be able to see the bird. I drove slowly, wanting the experience to last. When I arrived I took the bird out of the car and cleaned him carefully. The nurse said something as I entered the house, but I did not hear her. My mother said, "Oh," as I walked into the terrible room and turned to the spot where he always was. His eyes were shut but they opened now. For several seconds there was no recognition. I held the bird as high as I could and said, "I got him." My father's eyes found the bird and he raised his fist in silent celebration. It was his last conscious act. Shortly after my visit, he fell into a coma. He died nineteen days later.

My father was not a hunter, but he supported my love of the field. He would tease me about my allocation of time, money, and effort, but there was a respect that would occasionally find expression when he talked to his New York business associates about my determination and skill in the field. I will always believe he enjoyed the last gobbler he saw and the benefits it provided for his son.

·17

CAMOUFLAGE

The only time a hunter in full camouflage does not look like an absolute fool is when he is carrying an adult gobbler. Since most of us do not make a habit of carrying wild turkeys, we grow accustomed to looking foolish.

My partner once had an experience, however, in which the camouflage he sported resulted in his being perceived as something more threatening than a fool. Gary was driving back to town after an unsuccessful spring morning. In his rush to make a nine o'clock meeting, he had not yet removed any of his camouflage gear, including face paint, camouflage hat (complete with artificial leaves), and shooting glasses (with camouflage tape over the bottom half of the lenses). He hoped no one from the university would see him before he made the refuge of his home.

Encountering our town's one major intersection, he stopped to allow the traffic to cross. The third car that passed was driven by a high school student on her way to school. The girl's eyes found Gary's vehicle and, unfortunately, Gary. Horrified by the camouflaged figure, she lost control of her vehicle, which bounced up on the curb. Thankfully, the car was moving very slowly, and it came to a rough but not injury-inducing stop. Gary jumped out of his Scout to see if he could help. As he stepped on the pavement, he realized that in anticipation of the quick change at home, he had kicked his boots off and was now in complete camouflage except for white athletic socks. Gary's stature contributed to his strange appearance. He is only five feet four inches tall, but as a former wrestler, he has the upper body and arms of a much larger man. When Gary reached the girl's car he asked, "Are you all right?" The girl slid across the front seat away from him and screamed, "Stay away from me!" Confused, Gary turned to greet several men who had come to help. They stopped in their tracks, and one said, "Are you an American?" Gary tried to explain. "I've been turkey hunting," he said as he attempted to rub the green, brown, and black paint off his face. Without the benefit of cold cream, the colors merely smudged.

One man was staring at his shooting glasses, and Gary said, "I put the tape on the glasses so they can't see my eyes." The man said, "So *who* can't see your eyes?" Gary replied, "The turkeys." Two of the men stepped back and began whispering to each other. Gary desperately added, "This is camouflage. I wear it so the gobblers can't see me." One of the men was now staring at Gary's feet. Gary glanced down at his white socks and began to wonder if he could make it back to his Scout before they grabbed him. Gary said, "I'll call the police from my house." Without looking back, he ran for his vehicle. Feeling very insecure, he waved at the men as he headed through the intersection. No one acknowledged his wave. The men simply stared. Finally, one said, "Homer, you call Chief Arbogast and tell him some kind of English-speaking dwarf in combat gear is driving south on Route 11. He's in a red and white 1982 Scout, and the little bastard is armed!"

18

A DAGGER IN THE BACK

It has happened to me seven times. Each was a terrible experience. On every occasion I used my years of turkey hunting experience to select what I thought was the perfect location from which to call. Each time, I had a precise fix on the location of the gobbler. Dressed in state-of-the-art camouflage, and aware of the need to stay motionless, I had the bird responding aggressively to my calling. All the cards were in my hand. Yet in every case, the love-crazed gobbler somehow was able to sneak in on me and *stick a dagger in my back.*

What each great bird in fact accomplished was to get within fifteen feet of me before I saw him and lock on to me with his unforgiving eyes. All I could do was to attempt to throw my gun up quickly—and that *never* works.

Why some birds do not come directly to you is a question only they can answer. Some innate sense of caution, perhaps ingrained by close calls with hunters, teaches them to exercise a special type of wariness and *stalk* the hunter who is making the call. Does the bird that stalks you know that your call is an imitation? I do not think so. I am sure that some particularly wary birds—which have earned their wariness by encounters with hunters—occasionally make the same kind of cautious approach to a hen.

I suspect the dagger-in-the-back experience does not often come after a hunter has killed a bird and is relaxed. Each time one has done it to me, it has come when I *needed* a bird. The first was on my initial trip to the great turkey-hunting state of Alabama. It was the first day of my trip and I wanted to show my gracious hosts that I was competent. It was the only chance I got in three days. It hurt. On that occasion my host put me in a spot where I suspected he knew a gobbler had been roosting. At dawn the bird gobbled once. I made a few light calls, but he never responded. Twenty minutes later I saw movement ninety degrees to the left of the direction from which he had gobbled and where I was facing. He was looking right at me from twelve feet away. I threw up my gun. I am not proud of having let him stick the dagger in me, but I am pleased that I didn't try the going-away shot with the big 10-gauge at twenty yards. At least I hadn't compounded the situation by crippling the bird.

The second time one got me was when I was recovering from my third spinal surgery. I was not sure I could make it through the season. This was the sixth day I had hunted, and I desperately wanted the bird. He came in without a sound. When he flushed from fifteen feet away I would have been no more shocked if he had stepped on a land mine.

The last time I took a dagger was in 1997 when I returned to Virginia after a sabbatical in Chile. I had picked up some kind of parasite in South America, and for a while I had felt such intense pain in my stomach that I thought I was having a heart attack. The pain had diminished after two weeks, and I *needed* a bird. The first day that I felt good enough to hunt, one stuck a dagger in my back. I had been calling from a small saddle, and a hot gobbler was coming toward me. He gobbled constantly, and I made the terrible mistake of reflecting on how easy it can occasionally be. As he came up the slope, I *knew* he would come right into the open saddle to look for the coy hen. I looked down the rib of my gun and waited for him to appear. I wasn't too worried when his gobbling ceased; I was sure he was simply too busy making the final steep climb up the ridge. After five silent minutes, I began to wonder. At the ten-minute mark, I was worried. After fifteen minutes, I was a wreck. I tried a couple of light clucks—nothing. I stared into the saddle. Suddenly there was a loud *putt* from directly *behind* me! The next sound was the violent flush of the huge bird from ten feet away. I turned to see him rocket down the mountain. His dagger was in my back.

When you reflect on the skills turkeys have at locating you, do not forget the fact that they cannot smell you; they lock onto you with vision and hearing alone. I am not an elk hunter, but I cannot imagine that a bull could get as good a fix on you as these guys can. Their ability to determine the precise spot from which a call has come is uncanny, and it is not affected by their own movement. No matter how many times they turn and move after they have last heard you call, they know precisely where you are.

As stalkers they have no peers. They can move through a relatively dense hardwood cover without a sound. They also have a remarkable ability to use the lightest cover to conceal themselves. Each time I have been surprised by a stalking bird, I have retraced his steps and been dumbfounded that I was unable to see him.

At times I have had a bird put a dagger in my back even after I had devised a special strategy for him. Four years ago I was trying to fool an old gobbler that usually roosted at the top of a large hollow. After a couple of failures with normal techniques, I decided to set up at what I thought was his strutting area, make only one call, and then wait. I placed myself above the little flat with my back to the area where the bird roosted. He obliged by gobbling at dawn, and I made one series of soft clucks. He gobbled back aggressively and then went quiet. I was sure he was coming, but I didn't know if he would come around my right side or my left. As I sat looking away from the gobbler, I had the sense he was stalking me. I didn't like it. I strained to hear his footsteps in the leaves, but there was no sound. After ten minutes, I realized I was sweating and feeling vulnerable. I wanted to turn around and look up the hollow, but I knew he was waiting for any movement. *I became the hunted.* Time passed slowly. After half an hour, I couldn't stand the pressure. I had to make a call. I made a soft cluck with my mouth call—and it was all he needed. I never saw or heard him but he, too, put a dagger in my back.

I think about the war games people play. You want a real war game? Consider a mature gobbler armed. If they can stick a dagger in your back, think what they could do with a paint gun. In the fall a human wouldn't have a chance. Turn the hormones on in the spring and you would still be at terrible risk. How does the stalking skill of a mature gobbler compare to that of your average stockbroker? Let Michael Jordan go one on one with the worst kid on a junior high school basketball team and you might have an instructive comparison.

I have never hunted dangerous game in Africa, but I have often reflected on what type of threat a wild turkey would pose if he could hurt you. You think a buffalo is dangerous as he hides in wait after being seriously wounded? Try the tenacity, stealth, courage, and cunning of a wounded gobbler. If he had claws, horns, or teeth, you would be insane to hunt him.

Or if you want to add a little spice to your next turkey hunt, consider the threat the turkey coming to you would be if he carried a real dagger.

19

RED DOG

During the years when turkey hunting was coming to dominate my life, I read everything I could about it. I encountered articles on dogs used exclusively for wild turkeys. Most of these pieces were written in the early part of the twentieth century, and many were set in Virginia. The specialists were usually offspring of pointing dogs that had the speed and range to find flocks and scatter them. They also had the discipline to lie quietly at their master's feet as he called the scattered birds back.

The concept of training a dog to stay motionless in a blind was sobering, but Red Dog could do it. Now, she is not named Red Dog; her official name is Henry's Fork Sage. The nickname was applied by a good friend, Mary Virginia Myers, who babysat my wife when she was a child and now helps us with my mother. You have to hear Mrs. Myers say "Red Dog" to get the full impact of the term. When she says it, you have a sense of a *big* dog. And at ninety-five pounds, Sage is not petite. I understand that I am biased, but I think Chesapeakes are the most attractive of the retrievers. I also enjoy the fact that they are native Americans. The fact that I have Maryland roots, and that my parents and all my grandparents came from Baltimore and loved the Chesapeake Bay, may contribute to my affection for Chesapeakes.

Sage has the tenacity, courage, intelligence, temper, and independence that define the breed. She came from Idaho, where the harsh winters have made Chesapeakes popular. For years I avoided looking at Chessie puppies, because I didn't think I had the training skills to cope with one, but every time I came across a picture of a Chesapeake I got the urge. Finally I made the decision.

My start with the Red Dog was not auspicious. I took the puppy dove hunting with my partner. She ate the first dove she picked up. And when I say "ate," I do not mean she chewed on the dove—I mean she *swallowed* it in one gulp and then burped. I talked to her about the transgression, and she brought the rest of them to me without incident; however, the rest of the day Gary provided a nonstop monologue about the "dove-eating breed."

In the waterfowl blind she does not have the manners of a field trial dog, but crippled birds rarely escape. On her first eventful day on Henry's Lake she swam out of sight to retrieve a goose, then greeted a game warden by growling as only a Chessie can. She survived both experiences.

Her breeder told me that she was not sure Sage would "tolerate" a kitten my daughter wanted to bring into the home. In fact, she said, the Red Dog's ancestors had a history of killing cats. But with guidance the kitten soon became a good friend, and now we often find Sage and the tiny cat curled up together on the couch. At times the cat scares me with the liberties she takes with the huge dog.

When I want to impress someone with the strength of Chessies, I arrange to have them in my company when I feed Sage a bone. Chesapeakes do not chew bones, they *crush* them. To make the demonstration impressive, I give my pointing dogs bones at the same time. They lie down and contentedly chew while Sage crushes the bone, swallows it, and begs for another. I have never had a witness who was not impressed, if not frightened, by the act.

You have to see a Chessie withstand intense cold to appreciate what the breed can endure. On Christmas Eve 1997, for instance, I took Sage out on the Henry's Fork when the thermometer read four degrees below zero. She retrieved two mallards, two pintails, and three goldeneyes in half a day on the river. She was as eager to make the last retrieve as she was the first.

Sage will not win any Miss Congeniality awards. In fact, one of the more embarrassing experiences I have had with her involved a member of our faculty who had recently lost her husband to cancer. The colleague had a dog, and one day I saw them walking together. Thinking that dog talk might be a modest help for her, I called to show her my Chessie pup. This was my first experience with the "vehicle-protection" phenomenon. To my deep embarrassment, Sage did everything in her power to get out of the car and attack my friend's tiny dog. Nothing I said to Sage brought her out of attack mode.

A less embarrassing vehicle-protection incident involved a cross-country trip. A truck driver did not appreciate the Red Dog growling at him when he got close to our car at a rest stop. Sage was not growling aggressively—simply telling the guy not to come too close to my two daughters. The truck driver stuck his face against the window and cursed and screamed at the Red Dog. Sage, defining the man's act as a threat to the girls, turned on her Full-Fledged Chessie Attack Posture complete with slobber, shaking muscles, bared teeth, bulging eyes, and attack growling. The man fell over backward, screamed "Jesus Christ," and half crawled, half ran back to his truck. How the dogs are taught to protect property with such intensity is probably not a story any of us wants to know.

I had an even more impressive experience with the protective instincts of the Red Dog. It took place the day before our fall turkey season opened in 1997. I had Sage out to see if we could find and scatter a flock. I did not carry a firearm, since the season was not open. In our first tough hour we saw no sign as we walked in the rain. At the ninety-minute mark, we were high on the mountain in open hardwoods. My spirits were low because the acorn crop had been poor. I began to reflect on where else we might find birds when I saw Sage jerk to a stop. In front of her, not thirty feet away, was a black bear. As I watched, two large cubs appeared from behind their mother and climbed up a small tree. The mother looked at the cubs, then turned to me and the Red Dog. After pondering us for a second, she came for us. There was no growling or aggressive posturing. She just moved quickly, with her rolling gait, right toward us. The hair on the Red Dog stood up, and she walked out in front of me to meet the bear. I remember yelling something stupid like, "Come here, Sage!" My voice, and no doubt fear, kept me from remembering hearing any sounds coming from either the bear or the dog. The two animals faced each other nose to nose for several seconds—and then the bear turned and ran. Sage did not pursue her. I looked up at the two cubs, which were attentively watching their mom race off. I remember thinking that the mother bear had seemed smaller than I would have expected, and the two chubby cubs larger. I grabbed Sage, put her on the leash, and half ran, half stumbled down the mountain.

Sage can be wonderfully gentle and warm. She loves to ride in the passenger seat of my car and will continually reach out to touch me with her paw. She also puts her big head in my lap and sighs contentedly. In the house she lies at my feet for hours. In my office students always comment on Sage's gentleness and the fact that, despite my gruff commands to stay in her corner, the Red Dog will always have her head in the student's lap by the time the meeting is over. She *needs* human contact. When I have to keep her in a kennel, I know she suffers. She does not complain, but it is clear she misses the interaction with her human friends.

The Red Dog has learned the turkey game, and enjoys going after the big birds. She does not have the speed or range to compete with the fast pointing breeds in covering ground, but she will find a flock and scatter them. It is her intelligence that sets her apart. She knows she must stay quiet when in the blind.

I do not cover her with a blanket, the way a friend does to keep his "turkey dog" from jumping up at an inappropriate time. (I would respectfully suggest that anyone who *considers* throwing a blanket over a Chesapeake should seek help.)

If a bird is crippled, no pointing dog is a match for Sage. I certainly will make no claim that a Chessie is superior to any of the other retrievers at finding crippled birds; however, I will argue that no other breed *protects* a bird the way a Chesapeake will.

Sage once had a nice relationship with a big English pointer a friend owned. This pointer was a tough, rawboned male and I really believed he was a match for Sage. At times he had the temerity to growl at the caged Chessie. All was fine until the pointer flushed a small flock of turkeys, and I killed one as it flew back over us. Sage, who had been close to me when the pointer got into the flock, ran over, grabbed the bird by the wing, and struggled to pull him up the hill to me. Bob—all pointers have terrible names—came rushing down the hill, filled with the thrill of having scattered the huge covey of strong-smelling birds. His excitement made the fast dog even faster; he must have been going twenty miles an hour when he hit the Red Dog. The sound of the collision would have made the N.F.L. proud. Both dogs were stunned by the impact, and there was an instant of calm before the Chesapeake assaulted the big pointer. He tried to defend himself, but he was no match for the powerful Sage. After a frantic several seconds, the badly mauled pointer ran crying up the mountain. The Red Dog turned around to look at me, and then picked up *our* turkey and carried it to me.

I use the Red Dog as a beast of burden. The pack I got for her was designed for yuppie campers and their goldens, but it works for us. I stuff it with extra shotgun shells and other equipment that will not be broken if the dog should tumble down a slope. I can get about five pounds' worth in the pack. I don't miss the extra weight, and the Chessie doesn't seem to notice it.

Sage makes mistakes. One morning we returned to hunt some old gobblers I had scattered. Earlier in the season my partner and I had killed one gobbler from the flock, and that bird had taken more than four hours to come to us. I was sure the wait would, again, be a long one.

After settling in the blind, I made one short series of clucks. Immediately, I heard the sound of walking. I saw Sage turn her head toward the sound as well. I thought, "Too soon for a bird; it must be a hunter." The two-stepped gait was regular and headed up the ridge toward us. I saw Sage out of the corner of my eye and noticed that her tail was wagging. I knew it had to be a man, because when a turkey comes to the blind she goes rigid with intensity. I quickly grabbed my blaze orange hat, stood up, and held it high for the hunter to see. The footsteps were now so loud I could not believe the man was not visible.

The *huge* gobbler did not miss the hat as he crested the ridge. I was still waving it at him as he flushed. I swear the Red Dog cringed and put her head between her paws when I looked down at her.

20

NELL

Nell is my wife, best friend, and most respected adviser. If this chapter is perceived as a simple thank-you to a generous wife, it will be a dismal failure. I write about Nell not because her support has allowed me to become a competent turkey hunter, but rather because her story, and those of other women who remain anonymous in a culture oriented toward men, deserves to be told. This piece *is* relevant to turkey hunting. Any successful, passionate hunter who is married *will* have a spouse who is supportive. The importance of support from a spouse is a story as old as hunting.

Nell grew up in west-central Virginia where her father taught biology at Virginia Military Institute. Her parents were from Southside, Virginia, and they identified with the South as only Virginians can. Both her father and brother were hunters, and she grew up seeing the sport as something men did. Like many activities deemed to be exclusively within the domain of males in the traditional South—including football, war, and making money—hunting was not for women.

Before entering college, my wife accepted the roles that had been attributed to women in the South. The world was run by men, and the great ones were kind and generous to their lovely wives. Great men were effusive in their praise of their women's beauty, industriousness, and skills as hostesses and mothers.

In college Nell's insatiable reading generated questions about the values instilled by southern culture. She was bothered by the South's record in the realm of civil rights and began to see the popular history of the region as being highly selective—focusing obsessively on military heroes and eliminating certain populations, particularly blacks, from consideration. She also began to listen to those who were suggesting that there were roles for women outside of the home, nursing, and elementary school teaching. All of these ideas had entered her mind before she met the Yankee anthropologist.

My daughters are ready to rebel if Nell or I ever offer to tell the story of how we met. When they see it in print, they might not speak to me.

I was 30 when I started teaching at Washington and Lee. Nell was twenty and a student at Randolph Macon Woman's College in Lynchburg. She was a junior and had made the decision to spend her junior year at Washington and Lee to study under several superb English professors. Nell took no anthropology until the last semester of the year, but I had heard about her. One of the best students I had in my first semester was a very bright young man whose father was the chaplain at Virginia Military Institute. One day he asked me if I had met Colonel Reeves, a biologist at VMI. He said Reeves had done a lot of archaeology and taught an anthropology course. I found the young man's final comment to be particularly interesting. "Yes, and the colonel's eldest daughter, Nell, is the most beautiful girl in Lexington, and she is taking courses here this year. Too bad for all of us—she is engaged." I remember thinking that I hoped to meet her.

As I prepared to meet my archaeology class at the beginning of the spring semester, I was excited even before I saw her name on the roll. When I entered the classroom a beautiful girl—conservatively dressed in a skirt and blouse—offered a striking contrast to the shabbily dressed members of the lacrosse team who had signed up for the course after hearing I had played the game.

The young man had not exaggerated Nell's beauty. I was very sensitive to the ethical dilemma of a young professor finding a female student attractive. I also remembered the comment about her being engaged. So I just taught, enjoyed her presence, and hoped she liked the course.

Midway through the semester, I was handing back papers. She had done a great job. I pulled all my courage together to compliment her as she left the class. She was pleasant but seemed rather distant in responding to my comments. When I later returned to my office, her father called to offer an apology for his daughter. She had been suffering from a migraine headache, he told me, and in her embarrassment over her illness was rude when I talked to her at the end of class. I said she had not been rude at all, and hoped she felt better. I put the phone down and wondered.

I did not have the courage to initiate another conversation with her for the rest of the semester. The day after the class concluded, I called her at home, in abject terror, and asked if she would like to have dinner to "talk about the exchange program." This excuse was so weak even her younger sisters laughed about it when she told them. I actually called her back the day before we were scheduled for dinner to suggest that rather than going out, as I had originally suggested, she might consider having dinner at my home, as I had caught several brown trout and believed they would prove better than anything we could find in Lexington. She agreed, and we had a wonderful evening. The only subject we did not discuss was the exchange program. She pointed that out to me at the end of the evening. I learned her mother had been appalled at the idea of her having dinner at the home of "that Yankee bachelor."

Nell was also admired, and courted, by agemates from VMI as well as Washington and Lee. The second time I went to her farm, the house was filled with attractive young men. I felt insecure, but did agree to join in a volleyball game. One huge, athletic-looking guy seemed to be trying to kill me with the ball; I guessed that he may not have liked the idea of Nell dating a small professor. I saw Nell respond to the guy's attempts to decapitate me, and I had a sense she was on my side. As it turned out, she *was* on my side, and she has stayed there—no matter what the price.

We were married a year after I asked if I could talk to her about the exchange program. I've always been outspoken, and we had some problems adjusting to the expectations of our different cultures as well. For starters, I did not go to church. That was terribly hard for Nell's family, and I understood and appreciated their position. I was not sympathetic to the fact that concerns were raised when I said I hoped some black friends would make it to the wedding. It was clear that this was deemed inappropriate. It was easy for me to stand my ground, however. The beautiful young woman who had seen her family as a refuge against the world stood by me on all the tough calls.

From the start we recognized that despite our varied upbringings, we shared similar values. I believe she would agree that the most critical one was honesty. We have always been completely honest with each other. Now I hear Nell counsel our elder daughter, "Make sure he is honest and has the same values—that will be the key." She is right, but I still wonder how our values came together from such different backgrounds.

I believe a tremendous love for the natural world and a sense that all representatives of all cultures are equal were critical. Nell and I have both fallen in love with remote areas, and with the untamed people who have been part of the wonderful adventure that has been our life together. We didn't have to go to Coihique, Alice Springs, Loen, Te Anau, or Smithers to find these characters. We live with them each summer on the banks of the Henry's Fork.

Animals, particularly dogs, have always been a weakness—and Nell and I have shared love for many dogs. She teases me that she sensed early on in our relationship that she was of lesser status than a couple of the dogs. (Clearly a distortion!) I always enjoyed the relationship Nell had with our dogs; until the children came, they dominated our lives. The dogs fell in love with Nell. I can still remember the oldest moving to her to seek her gentleness after I had been harsh with him.

I have friends who enjoy reflecting on the women in their lives. One of the comments I hear is, "She was the most beautiful woman I ever dated; I wouldn't trade her for my lovely wife, but she was the number one looker." Or, equally sensitive, "Mary might not be in the top four in looks but she is my choice. Right, honey?" For the record, I never dated a woman who came close to being as beautiful as Nell. My father, watching Nell walk gracefully along the beach on Ocracoke Island, said, "Nell is a beautiful woman, and she will get more beautiful as she ages, mark my word." He didn't get a chance to see her striking gray hair but, as usual, he was right.

The trust and respect we share makes life together wonderful. It may be old fashioned, but I just love to be with her. To me she is more beautiful and exciting now than when I first met her.

Her attractiveness has been a bit hard on me from time to time. On three occasions while we were traveling, Nell was asked to participate in the filming of advertisements. Twice she was asked at airports, and once at a fishing lodge. On all three occasions the males selected to be seen with her were not her husband—who was available! I made note of the fact that each time the guys picked were Mediterranean looking and significantly larger than her short husband. On one occasion she was picked to play the role of George Marshall's young wife at a documentary being filmed at VMI. I thought I had the right hair color for the young Marshall, but they picked a handsome senior cadet.

The town in which we live will never have a powerful chapter of NOW. It is a town dominated by the memory of men who won fame in war: Lee, Jackson, and Marshall. Civility, grace, and impeccable manners are prominent everywhere you turn, but the two schools have historically denied women equal opportunities. VMI's protracted and poorly argued fight against coeducation remains compelling evidence of how far the South has yet to come.

Nell has grown accustomed to having men assume she lacks talent in those many realms that the culture of the South considers the exclusive domain of males. When contractors come to our house, for instance, it is always fun to watch them slowly recognize that the attractive woman is the one with the most intelligent questions. These men have been trained to talk only to other men, and it takes them time to adjust. Some never do. Nell is very good with mechanical problems; her husband is not. One man accustomed to talking only to the "man of the house" was unable to address Nell; I had to act as interpreter. His culture had taught him that beautiful women do not tell you where the electrical outlets will be placed. Nell in turn was raised to celebrate and exaggerate the accomplishments of men. It has been easy to show her how often we can be wrong and how frequently we need to be helped and supported.

While Nell is patient with those who assume her ignorance, she has taught her daughters not to be. Our elder, who graduated from Haverford College in Philadelphia—where the Quakers have been treating women as intellectual equals for years—is ready to start on a graduate career, and it will not be in elocution. At the age of fifteen, Liz—all five feet, one inch of her—interrupted a large dinner party that included faculty members, administrators, students, and alumni by snapping, "That is *bullshit!*" at a twenty-three-year-old Washington and Lee graduate who was asserting that women were not qualified to be physicians. Her mother, the most gracious hostess I have ever seen, smiled and let the embarrassed young man attempt to defend his indefensible position against the tiny girl with the heart of a badger.

Our younger daughter is an accomplished fly caster. She has learned that boys in our culture are taught to believe they can do everything better than girls. Once, at a fishing lodge, I watched a young man of my younger daughter's age try to show off by casting on the lawn. He was terrible. The kid turned to her and asked, "Would you like me to show you how?" Unfortunately for him, Cath had taken Mel Krieger's fly-casting course at the age of nine. She can double-haul seventy feet of line with the little 4-weight Winston rod that Tom Morgan made for her when she was ten. The kid gave Cath the rod and stood behind her, ready to help. I turned to Nell and saw the fierce smile. The young man learned a lesson: Do not make assumptions about the lack of skills of American women.

I have seen female courage—which in our society has never received the accolades given to the more selfish heroism of men. When our daughters were fighting psychological problems as adolescents, it was Nell who had the courage to make the tough decision to take one out of school, and to put another on a medication. We went through the tough times with our children together, but I always thought she was at the point, more effective, more aggressive, and more courageous.

Nell has seen me undergo major spinal surgery three times. She knows enough biology to recognize what can occur during eight hours of surgery on your cervical vertebrae. Our kids were very young at the time. She was strong, calm, and positive. She held up through all the ordeals—including having to bandage me twice a day for six months after one of the operations—with unwavering support.

She has not allowed anyone to take a cheap shot at her husband. Once, for example, I gave a talk for the university in Easton, Maryland. Many of the alumni in the group were of my era, and I heard one guy say to Nell, "Did you know we all called Johnny 'Stumpy' because he was so short?" I laughed, and expected to hear her chuckle as well. Instead, I saw the green eyes go cold as she said, *instantly,* "I heard on the lacrosse field you called him an All American." The irony of Nell's response was that I knew she thought the athletic distinctions I had received were meaningless; she teased me about the area in my bachelor home where I displayed team pictures and individual honors. She called the area my "shrine" until, sufficiently humiliated, I took the pictures and clippings down and put them into the attic.

It is such a joy to enjoy the same things as a spouse. Many of my friends take separate vacations, with the husband going

West to fish while the wife goes to the coast with the kids. Nell and I both love the rivers and the light and the people that are the West. At the same time I am proud of her quilting. As is the case with most artwork produced by women in America, the fabric crafts never get the recognition they deserve. The great female artists do not become discouraged or bitter, however—they just continue to produce great products that men ignore.

I know Nell shares the thrill I derive from wild turkeys. She says she feels the excitement when Gary and I are running around like six-year-olds getting ready for some adventure in the field. She not only shares in it, but she also respects the competence we have developed.

Once, after a long day of fishing the Henry's Fork with a guest, I stepped out on the porch of our cabin and spotted a huge rainbow feeding on the opposite bank. I suggested to my guest that he try the fish, but it had been a long day and he declined. I asked if he minded if I tried. Later, my friend told me that as he watched me wade across the river, Nell came up behind him and said calmly, "Keep watching him, because he will get that fish— it will just be a matter of time."

I do not always get the fish—but I feel her confidence every minute of every day.

21

KEEPERS OF THE FAITH

Many great hunters are what I call Keepers of the Faith. The faith they protect is not religious: rather, it is a code of behavior that is predicated on integrity, compassion, and hard work. The code says you must chase wild turkeys with an intensity that salutes their importance to your world. You must be aggressive, even relentless, but you do not take unfair advantage of them. You do not hunt them out of season, bait them, or shoot them in a field with a rifle.

The turkey hunter will only enjoy success by working hard. The Keepers of the Faith earn their successes and are unlikely to be obsequious. Every sycophant is dishonest. If you publicly agree with what the powerful say when you privately know it is wrong, you are a coward. You do not have to be on a battlefield to exercise courage. Try standing up for what is right when all the people around you are saying what they think the boss wants to hear. If you are able to convince yourself that it will do no good to fight tough odds, you have sold out. Every company man is a disgrace.

As a function of their refusal to exercise obsequiousness, Keepers of the Faith do not win many popularity contests. It is unlikely the county's best turkey hunter will be voted Teacher of the Year or Worker of the Month. It is not that he may not *be* the best teacher or worker, it just is that he will not have engaged in the politics necessary to achieve the popular recognition. In most cases the more gifted the hunter, the less likely he is to develop political skills. Turkey hunting keeps him honest. It teaches that only skill, determination, and toughness are rewarded. A turkey will not fall to the guy whom the boss's wife likes best. On most jobs, the Keepers of the Faith pay a price because they will not do or say what the powerful want to see or hear. Some have lost jobs, or failed to be promoted, because they were "too outspoken" (read "honest"). Today, in most professions, the obsequious get ahead. Many are very skilled at forming the alliances that allow them to prosper. I do not denigrate their skills. They are bright, bold, assertive, and tenacious. They are the ones who will get their wife a job in an area within the company for which she has had no training. They reap monetary benefits and prestige as they advance in their careers—but they will not be able to use their aggressive skills to cope in areas in which the measure of competence is pure, such as in the pursuit of the wild turkey. The turkey selects those who earn their reputations. The Keepers of the Faith develop pride in earned competence.

Keepers of the Faith can come from any ethnic or racial group, and from any socioeconomic level. Their morality provides for a spirit of crosscultural respect. To the Keepers of the Faith, the great Bushman hunter is a hero—not a cute character you paternalistically "respect," but a *great* hunter who generates as much admiration as a superb performer in any realm of human endeavor.

The Keeper of the Faith is ethical and fair. He does not take unfair advantage of birds. Killing a turkey is only satisfying if it is done under a set of guidelines. Those rules are not always mandated by law. My aggressive partner provides an example of this spirit of fairness. Late one fall season I had taken a turkey,

134

but Gary had not. We were walking out of the woods after an unsuccessful attempt to call a bird when a young turkey flushed practically at our feet. Gary did not shoot. As eager as he was to kill a turkey, he did not take a shot that would have been unfair. He was living up to his role as a Keeper of the Faith.

The Keepers of the Faith maintain important values. One skilled gunsmith would not sell or repair handguns. He could have increased his annual income by working on pistols, but he refused. In his words, "They were made to kill people." His position was not popular with the local rifle club or the NRA, who suggested that "we" cannot afford to take a stand against any kind of firearm because it will result in *all* firearms being confiscated. George Schielke stood his ground.

Maintaining important values demands honesty—not part-time or convenient honesty, but the harsh, uncompromising honesty that says pistols have no reasonable role outside law enforcement. An assault weapon is just that, a *weapon,* and it should be outlawed along with machine guns, hand grenades, and land mines.

Keepers of the Faith do not exaggerate their accomplishments. I remember one very bright guy who astounded me with his stories of his fishing success on the Railroad Ranch. He always talked of taking eight to ten big fish a day. I believed it until I fished with him. That day he even exaggerated the size of the one fish he caught. Others picked up on the distortions. The final embarrassment came when a picture of the guy was published in the *Henry's Fork Foundation* newsletter with a fish that *clearly* was not as large as he said it was in the accompanying text. He was not a Keeper of the Faith.

All Keepers of the Faith love the creatures they strive to kill. Great turkey hunters are efficient killers, but that does not mean they lack compassion. The most efficient human predators I have known have also been the kindest and gentlest people. I have watched the toughest Keepers of the Faith repulsed by hunting videos that show graphic, slow-motion footage of animals being shot. Those who take some perverse pleasure from such obscene tableaux will not be Keepers of the Faith.

Most Keepers of the Faith have great compassion for animals. Dogs seem to instinctively recognize Keepers of the Faith and will move to them. Some make the mistake of seeing the kindness, sensitivity, and compassion as indicative of weakness. The Keepers of the Faith have the courage to be tough. They will be the first to take a stand, and the last to pull back. They make the best of friends, and the worst of enemies.

Advanced levels of formal education are not prerequisite to being a Keeper of the Faith. All are bright, but many are not well educated. Their problem-solving talents often do not fit the confines of the culturally biased tests that our society relies upon to assess intellectual skills, but introduce me to a *great* hunter—in the Kalahari or Kahokia—and I will show you a bright guy. The primary ingredient of greatness in turkey hunting is a wonderful problem-solving ability.

The Keepers of the Faith have a quiet dignity. One is a turkey hunter who is obsessed with calls. I met him when he came down to look at my collection. When we talked, I sensed his honesty. He offered me an unusual call in trade. He said he had found it in an antiques mall and added, "I paid $125 for it." When he showed me the call, I recognized that I had, coincidentally, seen it in the antiques shop, and the price had indeed been $125. In every dealing I have had with him, this same pure honesty has been there. Roger once came through Lexington with his wife, and we had lunch. They talked about the challenges of raising children when both parents' place of work is far from their home. There were no complaints. At one point the wife talked about times when they had to eat cereal for dinner because of the lack of time. The quiet guy was quick to add that it was rare she didn't prepare a meal after the endless day.

The code of the Keepers of the Faith puts great value on loyalty. If a friend needs you, you are there. You salute the accomplishments of friends and acknowledge their talents whenever you have a chance. If your friend needs a recommendation, you will drop everything to help. You do not forget what others have done for you. Do not expect the majority of your associates to remember what you have done for them.

I know one remarkably successful businessman who could get *anyone* to work on a private project of his. But he found old friends whom he felt had the talents and created wonderful opportunities for them. Mike Monier of New York City and Jackson, Wyoming, did that between scheduling turkey hunts one spring.

Keepers of the Faith do not whine. Turkey hunting teaches you that it is not productive to complain. You learn to accept the failures and try again. Toughness becomes policy for the Keepers of the Faith. I remember the phone calls I have had with my friend Rich Tiberio, when he talked of the challenges of raising a son as a single parent with a modest income. I never heard a complaint; nor did he tell me the stories to elicit praise. He just did all he could, all the time, and I was awed by his sacrifices and commitments.

It would be wrong to imply that Keepers of the Faith have to be turkey hunters. The same qualities are found in honest, tough people from many backgrounds. As a young man, for example, Tom Morgan was one of the great fly-fishing guides in Montana. He had the foresight to buy the Winston Rod Company before everybody began to fly fish. In middle age he contracted multiple sclerosis. He is now confined to a wheelchair, but his closest friends have never heard him complain. Nell and I once had dinner with Tom and his wife, Gerri, at the Livingston Bar and Grill. An owner of a Montana fly shop came up to our table to speak to Tom. He addressed him as if he were a child. As the guy left the table, Tom flashed us his wonderful smile, with fire in his bright eyes, and said, "That dumb son of a bitch thinks the brain is a muscle." No laughter at the bar equaled the laughter that came from our table.

The elderly can be Keepers of the Faith. My mother will be one hundred on her next birthday. She has been in a nursing home for ten years. She and many of the other patients are women who have lived much longer than their more vulnerable husbands. They still laugh and face the immense challenges of old age in America with dignity. Many, like my mother, never complain.

Keepers of the Faith do not allow avarice to erode their characters. Keepers of the Faith are not going to cheat the little old lady out of her late husband's turkey call. They may travel five hundred miles to find the call, but they will pay her a fair price. Greed has created a subculture of the ruthless in our society. Some people seem to feel no commitment to honesty so long as the bottom line is impressive. You may argue that there is a very thin line between ruthlessness and aggressiveness. The line is nevertheless clear. Don't let the criminals tell you that every good businessman is ruthless. There are scores of tough, honest people who have not allowed avarice to make them evil.

I have had great students who avoided the temptation to follow the lead of their peers and make a fortune at any cost. Randall Ray was as talented a student as any I have taught, but he stayed in the Blue Ridge to play music and make instruments. In his quiet, self-confident manner, he knew his talents. He subsidizes his life of music and craft by painting houses. He had the courage to see what was important in life and refuse to compromise. He is a Keeper of the Faith.

Keepers of the Faith are generous, even though many are of modest means. One case in point is Pete. I met him when he showed up at our summer home in Last Chance, Idaho, in the tiny truck that served as his camp; some jerk had broken into his vehicle and stolen his camping equipment. I asked him to have dinner with us and lent him a few pieces of camping gear. We fished together, then had dinner. I learned a lot from him during our brief time together. It was clear the trip West had drained his limited financial resources. Yet he still found the dollars to join the conservation group that was protecting the river he loved. When he was about to leave, he told us to expect a package from him. The gift turned out to be a beautiful decoy. It was so much more than he should have done, but it defined Pete.

Keepers of the Faith destroy the stereotypes that have been built up about certain professions. Before condemning all attorneys as ruthlessly avaricious, listen to a story of one Keeper of the Faith, Bob Payne. Bob worked his way to the top of a prestigious law firm and then was appointed a federal judge. What you will not hear when the young attorneys talk about his exemplary career are the tough, time-consuming cases he took on without compensation. He did one for a widow, another for an uneducated black guy who worked in his college fraternity, and one for a friend who had been cheated by a contractor. Payne's loyalty and honor are complemented by competence and toughness. Do not tell me that the lead attorney in front of the cameras on the evening news is tougher or brighter than Bob Payne. I know better.

Keepers of the Faith work hard. In some cases their jobs may not be prestigious, but it doesn't matter; they work hard. The Keepers of the Faith carry their code of honor with them to their jobs. Each profession has its own form of "cheating." In mine, it is putting a few students in two different sections of a lecture course to give yourself credit for two classes; jamming all your classes into a few days so you have large blocks of time to do "your work"; designing tests and papers to be graded easily; showing films and videos instead of *teaching*; arranging your schedule so that as soon as exam week begins you can fly to Europe.

The cheaters will not be stopped. Why? Because the administrators need their votes to climb the ladder of success. Also, it takes *immense* courage to call a colleague a cheat.

In reflecting on the wonderful characters I have had the opportunity to salute as Keepers of the Faith, both those who hunt wild turkeys and those who do not, I realized that most have spent their lives with the same spouse. Fidelity and morality are important to them. It is a morality that extends to all realms of life. Some highly skilled hunters and anglers have no sense of moral boundaries. They feel you must be ruthless to be the best. The bottom line becomes the size of creatures they kill or catch, or the number of women who fall for their charms. They celebrate their immense appetites and use them as excuses for their abuses.

Do not think for a second that these moral, faithful, honorable characters I call Keepers of the Faith will be less capable or tough than the ruthless and immoral. On the contrary, the courage it takes to be honest and loyal selects for the toughest of them all. Beware of the faithful, unimpressive-looking character who puts a sign on his desk that says, THE BUCK STOPS HERE. They laughed at the idea that Harry S Truman could stand up to the toughest characters this great nation had produced. The ruthless and arrogant found out how tough Harry was.

It is important to acknowledge that the title Turkey Hunter does not itself make you a Keeper of the Faith. There are terrible stories about turkey hunters who stole the idea for a call from a bright guy who made a few in his basement and never had it patented. One common thief, who called himself a turkey hunter, found an article I wrote, changed the title, put his name on it, and had it published as his work. On the other hand, *great* turkey hunters are Keepers of the Faith.

Celebrate and treasure the Keepers of the Faith you find— and you will find these special people in both the most unspectacular and most prestigious domains of our nation. They will not look different. You will see their special qualities when courage must be exercised, when loyalty is needed, when a difficult decision has to be made. In such situations they will take a stand and provide examples for us all.

22

JAMES ON MATURE GOBBLERS IN THE FALL

He is of only average size, but something about the man attracts your attention. It may be the way he moves. He is no longer in his forties, but he moves as if he were twenty-five. He bounces up stairs. He walks at a rapid pace all the time, a relentless motion. Of all his physical features, the most defining may be his eyes. They are light blue, and they twinkle most of the time—occasionally, they look like lasers.

He is a gentle person. My children were at ease with him from the first time they met him. Dogs seem to recognize that he understands their place, and predicament. In the woods what sets him apart from most good turkey hunters is his intelligence. As they say on Madison Avenue, he is a very bright guy.

He has the requisite toughness. At fifty-three he can walk twenty-five-year-old men into the ground. He has the tenacity to hunt when he is hurt. Two years ago he pulled a muscle in his leg, and a physician told him he would miss the season. He wrapped his leg, hobbled up the ridges, killed two birds in two states, and never missed a day. I could see the pain in his face. When I asked him why he pushed himself so hard, he simply said, "That's part of it, John—you have to persevere." Such toughness endures. A lot of local hunters are successful early in the season, and then the strain gets to them and they just go through the motions. James is deadly on the last day.

He has developed and refined all the necessary skills. Some friends rave about his calling. He works at it and is never satisfied. I once watched him try to master a new type of call. I teased him and said, "Sandy Koufax didn't bother to throw a knuckleball—why do you need that strange call?" He looked up and asked who Koufax was. There is a lesson there. James doesn't waste his time with the distractions that make it hard for most of us to spend enough time mastering the skills.

He shoots very well. How good is he? Who knows? I have watched him break clay pigeons with boring regularity, but I am sure he would be no threat to the best European pigeon shooters. One thing I *can* assure you: If a gobbler makes the fatal error of showing James his head and neck at less than forty yards, the chances that the bird will survive the encounter are modest.

One thing that has always impressed me about James is that he listens. He is always attentive to my stories, no matter if they are about successes or failures. I believe he still learns from them. It may just be a function of his intelligence, but he is clearly a good listener.

He is also proud. There may even be a trace of arrogance. Once we went to listen to experts at a turkey-hunting seminar. The program was adequate, and the calling was excellent. One of the men must have weighed 350 pounds. I asked James what he thought of the show. He said, "They really are first-rate callers, John, no question about that, but I don't care how strong that fat boy is, there is no way he can hunt in our hills. Our gobblers won't accommodate fat boys." I laughed, but as he turned toward me, I could see the fire in his eyes.

The reputation that James has established has nothing to do with his occupation, his family, or his wealth. He has never won a calling contest, written a book, received a degree in wildlife biology, or been the master of ceremonies at a turkey seminar. He wouldn't be caught dead in cowboy boots or wear a turkey spur around his neck.

No one taught him to hunt. He learned the hard way. He knows what to do because he figured it out through trial and error. He has befriended a few of us by giving us advice. If we were lucky, he took us along and showed us how it should be done. He never tried to impress us with his skills; in fact, he told more stories about his failures than his successes.

He was always most intense when he talked about mature gobblers in the fall season. "They do not understand how difficult it is, John. I doubt if a tenth of 1 percent of the hunters of America are capable of successfully hunting mature gobblers in the fall. You have to be a little crazy, because there will be so many frustrating situations."

He continued in one of his all-time long monologues:

How do you hunt a creature that lives alone, in the most remote areas, is always alert, has incredible acuity of vision, and hearing, and an innate ability to sense danger? Unlike a large mammal, he can go for long periods of time with very little food. In the fall, his wariness is never compromised by sex. It makes spring gobbler hunting seem simplistic. There were periods of time when I thought it was just too tough— that they were essentially impossible to hunt. There is never a situation about which you can be highly optimistic. I cannot tell you how many times I have scattered a flock in the morning and stayed all day and not heard a peep. I have mustered the discipline to go back for the next two days and never seen or heard one of the birds. How much confidence can you muster the next time you scatter a gang?

I would be willing to bet that 95 percent of the mature fall birds killed are taken by chance. Some guy has one walk under his tree stand or one flies back over a hunter or one makes the mistake of crossing an open field and is assassinated by someone with a rifle. The number actually called or taken by some sort of strategy is very small. The contrast with the spring season is incredible.

Even when you do scatter a group and they make an effort to get back together, it will be a different process. In most cases they will reassemble in a location different from where they scattered and one that will give them good visibility for at least a hundred yards. You may fool them with the call, but they will make you come the last fifty yards to them. These gentlemen are not going to stick their heads up over the contour fifteen feet from you.

I respect the fact you do not like the rifle, John, but you should get a *good* Hornet and try it for a season on them. You cannot expect to call them to within thirty yards. The Hornet will give you a margin. I believe most of the great old-time fall hunters who specialized in gobblers used rifles.

James continued his discussion with a number of stories that substantiated his point that he, too, had often been frustrated by gobblers in the fall. The point he made repeatedly was that there were many times when he had no explanations for why he never saw or heard a bird after scattering a gang. He concluded the conversation by saying:

Also, when you write about me and the fall gobblers, don't let them think I have the answers—that would not be true. For every one I kill, I get outwitted by a bunch.

Tell them if they want the toughest hunting challenge in this world, old gobblers in fall is it. I haven't been to Africa, John, but you and I both know some boys who have killed the "big four" and there is no way any of them can deal with mature fall gobblers. I got into an argument with the radiologist after he went to Africa. I told him I could have killed every one of those animals with the old 270 if I had some of those solids. That one Englishman did it, John. I am sure he could shoot, but *so can I.*

Sometimes I wonder if the Indians had a special category for the hunters who could kill mature gobblers consistently in the fall. I wonder if some had the skill to do it whenever they wanted. Now, that would be a hunter. I would love to watch one of them and talk to him about it. Can you imagine that—I mean killing them *consistently* with a longbow and a stone point! I really believe they may have had that kind of ability. I hope you know, John, that that level of skill would make me look like a beginner.

23

SOUTHERN BOYS

I am not one, but as a function of attending college in the South, marrying a southern woman, and residing in Virginia for thirty years, I *know* southern boys. After more than three decades of interaction with them, I am sure our finest turkey hunters are from their ranks.

I was not prepared for the social skills of southern boys, nor their ease with women from the local girls' schools. At parties, they astounded me with their humor and ease. I am still in awe of their social grace and confidence with women.

As friendships developed during my first year in college, I learned that many of the boys were accomplished hunters. My first clues were the guns they owned. They *all* had classic American shotguns: Model 12 Winchesters, Browning Auto-5s, even old Parkers. Some of the guns had been handed down by fathers who hunted, but there were also wonderful stories such as the one of the 20-gauge Model 12 resting under the Christmas tree in the elegant Memphis home. By comparison, my northern boy-hood hunting companions had to educate their parents and then develop an effective strategy to ensure that *any* shotgun would be under the tree. It was not always a function of family wealth, either. Many of my adolescent friends came from families of means; the difference was that our fathers were rarely avid hunters.

One reason for this was the South's essentially rural resi-dence patterns. Southern boys were never far from good hunt-ing; for many, it was out the back door. My northern agemates were taken to Eagles or Red Sox games rather than to more dis-tant field opportunities. The kids who regularly went to Franklin Field or Fenway Park rarely had gamebirds in the backyard.

The opportunities in the South produced a tradition of hunting—and for many it became a passion. When I reflect on the finest game shots I have known, most have been southern boys. The bird seasons of the South played a role. As a kid in Pennsylvania, I was accustomed to a pheasant season that lasted for essentially a month—from the last Saturday of October to the end of Thanksgiving. The limit on pheasants was two a day, eight a year. Compare this to the opportunities of the southern boy, who started with doves the first Saturday in September and could still be chasing quail in February. At times the limit for doves was *eighteen* a day. With some imagination, and tolerant parents, you could shoot flying game every day for *five months.*

Southern women supported the addiction that southern boys had to the field. The successful hunter or fisherman was known to women in the South. I remember how surprised I was to hear well-educated southern women talk of the field skills of men. The women rarely hunted, but hunting was a respected part of the subculture of the South. The first day of any season generated an excitement that extended to the wives, mothers, and sisters of the hunters. The importance of hunting was *under-standable* to southern women. I have heard women from areas outside the South ask their men with obvious sincerity, "What is it that you enjoy about hunting?" That question would not come from a southern woman.

Before you decide to pack your bags and head South, let me talk candidly about southern boys. Most see women as essentially inferior to men. Southern gentlemen will expound on how attractive their women are, how dependent they are on them, and the indispensable value of their domestic roles. In practice most southern women have been denied power.

Honor is at the core of southern values. There is a spirit that the gentleman does not lie or cheat, and he does not tolerate companions who do so. My own education at one of the bastions of southern honor, Washington and Lee University, instilled this spirit in me. It was an important lesson. I remember the contempt I felt for fellow graduate students who cheated in a prestigious Ivy League graduate program. That experience was one of the factors that convinced me to return to the southern school to teach.

With maturity, however, I learned that the exercise of honor in the South was selective. Fraternity men were not held accountable for abusive behavior toward women. Women were put in categories based on the colleges they attended. If the school was not deemed prestigious, they were considered fair game. It was not called "date rape" at the time, but a lot of "gentlemen" engaged in assaults on intoxicated women. It took me more time than it should have, but I began to see an evil pattern. A young man might be instantly expelled for stealing a piece of beef jerky from a convenience store while drunk, but a classmate with a better pedigree would be allowed to graduate despite the fact that administrators knew he had assaulted a female.

The astute, ambitious administrator knows better than to tell the members of the board of trustees—the majority of whom reflect with fondness, if not sheer reverence, on their "wonderful years in the house"—that the fraternity system endorses sexism and alcohol abuse, and is contradictory to everything the institution should be about. Alumni do return to visit the houses and talk to the current members about how they need to be concerned about alcohol abuse; however, the instructions will often be offered in the format of: "Now, *you* boys have to be responsible; you can't afford to do what we did. Hey, have you heard about the time we tossed the piano out of the housemother's window?" After the current members finish laughing at the great story told by the wealthy man with the beautiful wife, they are told not to do all the cool things he and his buddies did.

Kids get killed in accidents related to alcohol abuse—try two from the same fraternity at Washington and Lee in a period of less then two years. Instead of taking a courageous stand against alcohol, the administration told us there "was a need for students to learn to use alcohol responsibly." I suspect the parents of the dead boys think the price tag for alcohol education was high.

Some of my southern friends have taken steps to address these problems. Others, also good friends of mine, will try to argue every point I have made. All is not perfect in the land of Lee and Jackson. No matter how critical I might be about southern honor, though, I have developed nothing but the greatest respect for the field skills of southern boys. Let me relate a couple of experiences that speak to those abilities.

CASE ONE

I invited two great turkey hunters to go goose hunting with me in Easton, Maryland. This was during the late 1970s when the Eastern Shore shooting was at its peak. Both guys had hunted most of their lives, but had never killed Canadas.

We stayed in one of the large motels that catered to hunters from the metropolitan areas in the Northeast. The first morning we walked into a large restaurant filled with goose hunters. Most looked as if they had been outfitted in the same shop or from the same catalog. A few men—generally younger, fitter looking, with worn clothes—were among the patrons. These were the guides. My two southern friends, Rector and Adams, didn't look like members of either group. Rector in particular was distinctively dressed in a pair of canvas duck overalls. As he walked between the tables, many of the men stared at him. If he was put off by the attention, he gave no indication of it.

When we met our guide, he seemed detached and unenthusiastic. He was clearly tired from too many early mornings of hunting, as well as the more draining demand of having to consistently produce geese. He answered our questions briefly, and complained of the problems that he and his associates had been having with geese that fed at night.

The large field we were to hunt was within 250 yards of a major road and surrounded by several small homes. As we drove into the field we immediately saw the decoys. There were hundreds of them, all covered with frost. At close range they were not impressive at all: Most were old tires or crude silhouettes. The one impressive aspect of the situation was the pit blind. It was large, deep, and well hidden.

After we lowered ourselves into the blind, our guide said, "Have you boys killed any geese?" When Adams and Rector said they had not, he responded with undisguised dismay, saying, "Shit! Well, then I'll be shooting, too." He did not ask us if he could shoot; he simply informed us he would. I almost said something about the fact that my friends were accomplished game shots, but decided against it. The guide also indicated that only he would watch the birds as they came to us.

The plan was to keep the pit uncovered until a group of geese was spotted at a distance. We would then duck our heads and slide the top of the blind over us. The guide would watch the birds through a small peephole. Once, the guide growled at me for tilting the lid of the blind to sneak a look at the geese. I remember hearing Rector laugh as I tried to peek out.

Several groups of geese gave us a look, but despite the guide's aggressive calling, they did not come in. The guide carried on a profane monologue of disgust with each group that failed to respond. Just when we were beginning to get accustomed to the rejections, the guide began to gasp between his calls, "These look like they may come. Get ready!" The wonderful sound of the birds came to us. When it sounded as if they were on top of the blind, the guide screamed, "Take them!" And we sprang up to a sky full of geese.

The limit that year was two a day. I am not sure how much the guide's assumptions about our lack of shooting skills influenced us, but I suspect it helped our concentration. More important, we had huge birds hanging right above us at point-blank range. For boys who regularly killed limits of doves with a box of shells, it was a slaughter. When the volley was over, nine geese were on the ground. The guide dropped his gun and jumped from the blind, screaming, "Oh my God!" as he frantically ran toward the birds while looking over his shoulder for the wardens I am sure he thought were watching. He stumbled and fell flat on the ground as he struggled back to the blind with four of the geese. He pushed himself up to a kneeling position and screamed, "You bastards, you killed more than the limit! I could lose my license!"

The two southern boys fixed him with cold stares. Rector said evenly, "Don't raise your voice. I can tell you which two geese I killed, and I know Jim and John can as well. I suspect you killed three, and you are the only person here who did anything illegal. We said we hadn't killed geese; we didn't say we *couldn't* kill them."

The look on the guide's face changed from panic to confusion and he did not respond. During the last couple of hours he spent in the company of the two southern boys, he was exceedingly polite.

CASE TWO

I was stationed at Fort Bragg, North Carolina, on orders to Vietnam. I had told some friends in Pennsylvania that I was going to Bragg, and they gave me the name of one of the old families of Fayetteville. I was invited to their home, and my visits became a wonderful escape from the army. Many of our conversations focused on the males' favorite game—wild turkeys. I never had a chance to wild-turkey hunt with them, but not long after meeting them, they asked me if I would like to join them on the first day of the dove season.

When I arrived at their home, I was sure the scene was comparable to Lee's headquarters before a battle. The huge and exquisite mansion was filled with energetic people. There was more food for the prehunt lunch than all the dove hunters in the county could have consumed. The women, most of whom were inexplicably attractive, were not only involved in the preparation of the food extravaganza but also responding to the endless requests from male family members looking for their hunting gear. The women harassed the men about their inability to keep track of their socks and shells, but the teasing was good natured and the women seemed to enjoy their roles. I watched the scene with rapt curiosity. The excitement did not keep the participants from being courteous to the bewildered Yankee dressed in the tiger-stripe camouflage. My dress made me feel foolish. The attire for the Home Force seemed to be Duck Head khaki pants, Lacoste alligator sport shirts, white cotton socks, and loafers.

I enjoyed the wonderful lunch. It was during the meal that the great humor of some of the participants came through. The patriarch of the clan worked in Washington in some important capacity, and he greeted me with warmth and good humor. As we ate, I marveled at his quick wit. After he had put me at ease, he loudly asked a son at the other end of the long table if the last Yankee who had hunted with them ever did hit a dove. The women shouted at him for his teasing, but his quick smile to me made it clear there was no mean intent. For the rest of the meal I was laughing too hard to eat.

The ride to the field was an adventure. The joking and laughter never ceased as the patriarch's eldest son drove the car with a combination of recklessness and skill. We were significantly over the speed limit most of the time, but I had a hunch we were unlikely to get pulled over. When we reached the huge cornfield there were twenty-odd vehicles gathered at one end. Again the scene was one of happy pandemonium. Men and retrievers engaged in their respective greeting and dominance-determining rituals. I was happy to see that some of the men had on camouflage clothing, but there were more who appeared to be outfitted for walking the beach at Hatteras. I stood on the sidelines as I watched a number of men come up to our car and greet my hosts. The greetings were filled with laughter, but there was a measure of deference, and I surmised that the commanding officer of this event had arrived in our vehicle.

As I pulled back from the loud teasing, I looked out at the field and saw waves of doves dipping across the corn. I suspected some measure of effort, and expense, had been invested to make sure there would be ample targets.

Soon the patriarch was telling people where to go. His instructions were accepted without comment. He teased several men—"I hope you practiced since last year!"—and was warm with several eager young boys who were going out for the first time. When he got to me, I braced myself for the requisite Yankee jokes but felt more confident when I heard him say, "Mr. *Mac-Daniel*, it would please me if you would go over to the big oak with Ashby." He added, for all to hear, "Mr. McDaniel is a captain in the eighty-second at Bragg and a guest of ours . . . and I have a suspicion he can shoot."

Ashby was nineteen and a student at Chapel Hill. He had on the basic uniform I have described above. The only alteration was a bright white tennis visor; and his alligator shirt was pink. Ashby was of average height, but a bit on the heavy side. He had not talked to me much during the pregame meal, and I felt a bit awkward as I walked to the back of the car with him. When I saw his gun, I heard myself exclaim, "Oh!" The blue on the gun was silver, but the raised rib, the figure in the wood, and the exquisite engraving indicated it was one of the few high-grade Model 12s I had ever seen. I commented on the gun and he quickly handed it to me, saying, "It was Daddy's first gun, nickel-steel barrels, made in the 1920s."

As I followed Ashby across the field, the familiarity with which he carried the gun and the way he gracefully moved it from one relaxed position to another were not lost on me.

Men were teasing each other at a distance as we waited for the appointed hour to arrive. My watch said a few minutes after noon when I saw the patriarch wave a flag. The sounds of shotguns filled the air instantly. Doves were everywhere.

Ashby stood in front of a big oak holding the Model 12 in his right hand, the gun upside down with the barrel resting on his right shoulder and pointing behind him. His left hand was casually stuck in his pants pocket. He looked totally relaxed, as if doves were the last thing on his mind.

I watched a small group of doves fly toward him. He did not move until they flared. In a blur, he flicked the gun off his shoulder, caught the fore end of the stock with his left hand, and smoothly tracked a dove; it exploded in a puff of feathers. An instant later another was frozen in the air. He then spun quickly to his left to take a high dove I had not seen. *All* the doves were still falling when he dropped his right hand from the gun and reached into his pants pocket for more shells. He looked up and down the field for more birds as he reloaded.

The rest of the afternoon was spent watching the finest wingshot I had ever seen perform his graceful magic. I marveled at his skill. Once, out in the field to retrieve a bird, he responded to a warning that birds were coming by dropping to the ground and lying flat on his back. He killed two from that position as they darted over him. On another occasion, a group that had already been shot at came flying low across the field straight at him. He killed the leader as it came dead-on, then pivoted 90 degrees to the right to take a second, then spun 270 degrees to the left to take a third.

The limit was eighteen in 1970, and after a while he began to pick his shots. He killed some at very long range. A dove is a tiny bird, and one at forty-five yards looks a long, long way off. Ashby understood how easy it is to overestimate how far away a dove is, and took some that were much more than forty-five yards from him. What made the performance so astounding was that I had assumed that his deadliness on birds at close range was a function of an open-choked skeet or improved-cylinder gun. I later learned that his gun was choked full. To shoot a full-choked gun well in a dove field takes several qualities: tremendous confidence, an ample measure of arrogance, and consummate wingshooting skill.

I have had the privilege to watch a lot of wonderful wingshots across this great nation. When I assess their skill, I always compare it to the fluid grace of the southern boy in the pink sports shirt standing on the edge of the corn, swinging the Model 12 with ease and speed.

24

BUTTERBALL

There are times when turkeys can be *impossible*. One fall I confidently asked my two daughters if they would each like to invite a friend for dinner to sample the wild turkey I was sure I'd kill during the week that preceded Thanksgiving. I *always* killed one. Because my girls had never celebrated Thanksgiving with a domestic turkey, the question was met with quiet approval.

You can guess the rest of the grim story. The young flocks were not where I expected them to be. Despite my best efforts, I had trouble finding sign, let alone birds. Several professional commitments took me out of the field for two or three days and the pressure began to build.

One evening at dinner Elizabeth said, "Daddy, we're not going to have to eat a *Butterball,* are we?" I said "I hope not" with a laugh, but when I looked at the calendar I realized I only had a few more mornings to hunt. One evening I finally scattered a flock of birds. The next morning a fine young gobbler came toward me screaming his head off. At a range of about fifty yards he encountered an old barbed-wire fence that ran through the woods. The bird made a detour along the fence, and I sensed that the jake would not cross the obstruction. In a state of anything but cool efficiency, I inexcusably took the long shot and watched in horror as the bird leapt into the air and flew off. The ultimate choke job. When I returned home, my explanation was met with a combination of disbelief and contempt by the two girls and their mother.

Somehow I knew my final two mornings would not be productive, either. The hunts were frustrating but not quite as bad as being called "Butterball" by my eleven-year-old and seven-year-old daughters. I had never realized how nice the term *Dad* was until then. The story of my failure spread faster than imaginable as my daughters told my friends about my failure.

The climax occurred when our sensitive, caring departmental secretary heard the story and I began to get "Butterball" notes tacked onto my office door. My phone message indicated that "Butterball" was not in his office.

We did eat a Butterball for Thanksgiving, and the girls seemed to enjoy their meal more than they should have. Their father learned an important lesson: Even young turkeys can be tough in the fall, and the arrogant anticipation of success is a sure strategy for humiliation.

25

CALL MAKERS

Among the first tools developed by hominids were those made for hunting, fishing, and gathering. There is evidence that our ancestors made stone knives and points more than one million years ago. We will not find turkey calls in Olduvai Gorge, but they have a rich history.

The earliest attempts to mimic game and birds were no doubt done with the human voice. It is probable that the first calling "tool" was a device designed to amplify a hunter's voice. My bet would be it consisted of a simple megaphone-type tube made of skin or bark. As in the development of all hunting tools, the effective hunter worked to improve and perfect his call. The process has not stopped. Today, bright people work to make better calls. When an advance is made, the word gets out. The path to the door of the creative maker is worn deep by fanatics like me.

The range of calls developed to reproduce the sounds of the wild turkey is fascinating. You look at a call, and you wonder how the idea to make it was generated. There are so many variations: boxes, slates, tubes, wingbones, trumpets, snuff cans, tortoise shells. . . . The endless list is a tribute to the innovative capacity of the human brain.

I shall provide a special tribute to three call makers: Raymond and Era Chisholm, and D. D. Adams. All are deceased. I have selected these characters because I believe they are representative of the makers who are at the core of this wonderful story. There are also distinctions between the Chisholms and D. D. Adams that will be instructive as we look at makers in general.

This is not my first tribute to the Chisholms. There are photographs of Raymond making calls in my book *Spring Turkey Hunting*. I selected them as representative of call makers once again because their story is a great one. As is the case with most of the great makers, the calls did not provide them with either fame or fortune. The two makers, Raymond and his wife, Era—who carried on the tradition after his death—were creative, honest, and independent. I see them, D. D., and the other great call makers as Keepers of the Faith.

If you find a Chisholm call and someone who knows how to use it, you will appreciate the couple's creativity. I would not hazard a guess at the number of wild turkey gobblers that have fallen to calls they have produced. The Chisholm call captivated me because of the ingenious nature of the design, the simple tools used to make it, and the remarkable tone it produces.

The Chisholm call works by friction. A striker made of a peg of wild magnolia wood is fitted to a hollow corncob. The end of the striker is pulled across a thin (one-eighth inch by five inches) strip of aluminum that is glued into a narrow channel in a hand-sized sounding chamber made of two concave pieces of wild magnolia wood. How Raymond Chisholm came up with this imaginative design remains a provocative mystery.

The turkey-call business is booming. A huge sporting goods store may stock more calls than the Chisholms' total lifetime production. Many mass-produced calls are of high quality and extremely effective. In some cases the type of call evolved with the company that markets the product. More frequently, what occurred was that a hunter who happened to be a crafts-man saw a call and used it as a model to make one himself. His attempt to improve the call seemed natural. The success of the modifications next caused local hunters to ask if the maker would produce one for them. As the popularity of the call grew, large-scale call manufacturers were attracted to the new prod-uct. If one thought the call had the potential to be marketed na-tionally, he would try to work out a deal with the inventor. In a few cases the inventor was given credit for his creativity and a mutually beneficial relationship established. Frequently, how-ever, the originator failed to protect his call with a patent, and suddenly a very similar call would appear on the regional or national market, with the inventor receiving neither credit nor financial reward.

Great products tend to be produced by people of integrity. The Chisholms didn't look like artists. There was nothing im-pressive about their appearance. They just looked like a couple of nice folks from Mississippi. They could have been reliable neighbors, the trusted farm couple. In truth, they were *artists*.

I never had the opportunity to speak to Raymond, but I would be willing to bet that you could sense his confidence. I've often wondered if his personality was comparable to those of other great call makers I have known. There is a pure confi-dence—a kind of gentle arrogance.

The late D. D. Adams was one of the great call makers of his era. His techniques, tools, and strategies provide an interesting contrast to the Chisholms. All were artists, but they operated in different ways. It is fair to say that D. D. was responsible for many of the advances made in slate and glass friction calls be-tween the early 1970s and the mid-1990s. Until D. D. began to practice his magic, the slate friction call had remained relatively static in design. There had been an evolution from the simple flat piece of slate and a striker; however, in the 1970s and 1980s D. D. experimented with various types of containers for his slate and glass surfaces. One of his most important innovations was set-ting more than one piece of slate or glass in his calls. These "dou-ble slates" became the rage of the period, and I can vividly remember the shock on the faces of good callers when they heard the remarkable tones for the first time.

D. D. was never satisfied with a call. The collectors of his calls can show their remarkable evolution. A comprehensive collection will demonstrate wide variations in materials and sizes of both the calls and their strikers. In fact, one of the exciting aspects of D. D.'s calls was that every time you thought you had a call that could not be improved upon, he would send you one that sounded better.

Unlike the Chisholms and many of the other great call makers, D. D. relied upon modern tools both to achieve closer tolerances and to do things, such as polish the surfaces of the glass calls, that simply could not be done with a penknife. The reliance on modern tools did not keep his products from being folk art, but simply allowed him to be more creative.

The Chisholms and D. D. Adams are representative of *all* the great call makers. Any list of makers will be incomplete; however, some names are as directly attached to the sport as *Winchester* and *Remington*. In some cases only a single word is necessary: for example, *Gibson, Lynch,* or *Kirby.* These three makers are associated with three distinct periods in the history of the sport. Gibson was the earliest, at the turn of the twentieth century: Lynch dominated the midcentury and the period when the sport was primarily associated with the American South: and Kirby emerges as the sport rose to national popularity in the 1970s.

Many of the most fascinating stories in the sport's history involve those creators who maintained a limited inventory of calls that they *alone* produced. This list is dangerous for me to offer, because every student of turkey calls will feel that someone has unfairly been left out. Accepting that fact, and yet determined to salute these important characters, I would have to include: Tom Turpin, D. D. Adams, Parker Whedon, Neil Cost, Ken Morgan, Frank Cox, Leon Johenning, C. H. Butler, Doug Camp, Bill Tannehill, Tiny Coiner, Zack Farmer, Tom Gaskins, V. O. Johnson, Mike T. Jones, John T. Miller Jr., Raymond Chisholm, Era Chisholm, John Pulley, Roy O. Rhodes, Charles Robinette,

Harold Shields, Richard Shively, Don Sitton, Lewis Stowe, Billy White, and Lamar Williams.

At the risk of angering most of the men I have included in the above list, I shall add that in my humble opinion there is an even more select group within their ranks that produced calls that became the standards by which all others were judged. This "best of the best" group would include Neal Cost, D. D. Adams, Ken Morgan, Frank Cox, Raymond Chisholm, and Parker Whedon. What distinguishes these makers is their special creativity, the remarkable tonal quality of their calls, and the aesthetic value of their products. A few in the group—Morgan, Adams, and Chisholm—placed more emphasis on innovation and practicality, while Cox, Cost, and Whedon produced calls that are not only functional but also works of art. Unlike many talented makers, none of them allowed greed to dictate mass production of an inferior product. Finally, these men were great turkey hunters. They all had paid their dues in the field.

I will add several sleepers to my list. These individuals either have recently started making calls, or their production has been limited. They are among the most talented of the makers. If you have a chance to find any of their calls, I suggest you grab them. The four are Rich Tiberio of Vernon, New Jersey; Ralph Permar of Old Zionsville, Pennsylvania; Earnie Fetters of Lewistown, Pennsylvania; and Dennis Poeschel of Milwaukee, Wisconsin.

It is important to recognize that in addition to the makers who have achieved fame or are in the process of becoming well known, there have been many makers who refused to do more than make great calls for friends. Some of these makers never allowed one of their calls to be sold. In such cases the wonderful products were obtained by only a few people. I have a friend who is one of these characters. A resident of the Blue Ridge Mountains, he earns a living as a barber. He has never allowed me to pay him for any of the calls he has given me. They are wonderful products, but Ken Kirby's lucky friends are the only ones who will know what a great maker he is. I know there are others out there like him who have kept their talents hidden. They, too, are important parts of our story.

There are men who, while not producing calls, are great call *tuners*. They can take good calls and, with modest alterations, make them great. The best I have encountered is Roger Parks of Pennsylvania. A devoted follower of D. D. Adams, Parks has a remarkable ability to alter friction calls so they perform more effectively. His skills were clearly developed by working with D. D. and Harold Shields in the area in which the great friction calls evolved. It is absolutely incredible what Roger can do with a call. His technique often involves aggressive sanding of the call's glass surface. There may be a little magic involved in the skills that both makers and tuners bring to their calls.

As a form of folk art, I believe turkey calls should be compared to waterfowl decoys. Today many communities—such as Havre de Grace, Maryland—have developed a significant tourism industry based on the waterfowl decoys that citizens of the town on the upper Chesapeake Bay have produced. The story is a great one because ordinary men—fishermen and merchants—produced decoys that now reside in the Smithsonian Institution with the other finest examples of American folk art. To each maker, the decoys were simply functional tools, but each man imposed his own special sense of how the bird should look. In addition, the style was influenced by earlier makers. Regional styles also developed, as they do in all forms of folk art. As with the Chisholms and D. D. Adams, some makers brought genius to the craft. The incredible Ward brothers from the Eastern Shore of Maryland are classic examples. If you know ducks, you must see at least one decoy produced by these two barbers. They are incredible. They come alive. They were carved and painted with simple tools by men who never benefited from formal art training. Somehow they capture the essence of the birds. The postures are perfect. They will stand with any sculpture in any museum in the world.

A call produced by Neal Cost, D. D. Adams, Ken Morgan, Raymond Chisholm, Frank Cox, or Parker Whedon is like a Ward brothers decoy. It is a work of art that is also functional. It will remain an important part of the American story. You don't stamp it out of plastic and make four thousand like it in a morning. You don't have to try twenty to find one that works. And yet no two are precisely the same. Call collecting has become a major pursuit for many turkey hunters. It has been very beneficial for our sport, because it has brought recognition to the great makers and helped stimulate the continued evolution of calls. Today, calls produced by the makers listed above are being purchased for six to ten times their original prices. I am told by men who should know that the six Neal Cost boxes I own could be sold for five hundred dollars each. I paid thirty-five dollars for the first I purchased in 1980. As is true of all folk art, those pieces deemed the most collectible are bringing phenomenal prices.

For many of us, what is so exciting is that we now have valuable collections that we established simply by buying calls for hunting. Every time we heard about a great call, we had to have it. Our considerable outlay of cash for those many calls—it will astound you how many calls avid hunters accumulate—was not for the purpose of collecting but simply to find more functional calls. That has changed. Now many people collect calls that will never be used in the field. It is an understandable evolution. Some of the most highly sought calls are so valuable that you would risk significant economic loss if you took one into the field. I love the fact some of us still hunt with highly collectible calls. I have been offered ten times what I paid for calls that I take into the field every day I hunt. That will not change.

You might logically assume that those of us with the most valuable calls would protect them more carefully than we did in the past. *Wrong.* We have *always* protected them carefully, because they were important to us before they became economically valuable. My favorite Chisholm and D. D. Adams friction calls were priceless to me even when I could have bought others of the same design for twenty-five dollars. The reason was that even the great masters could never be sure that any two calls would produce exactly the same tone. For example, D. D. once sent me striker after striker to try to get one that equaled the tone of the striker I had. Even using the same lot of wood and the same precise dimensions, the great craftsman could not do it. That is part of the wonderful mystery.

I am biased in favor of calls that were produced exclusively for hunting. In recent years highly decorative calls have been made by makers whose goal was more aesthetic than functional. That is fine, and you can see the parallel with decorative decoys. I love an attractive call, but if it does not have a good tone, to me it is not a great turkey call.

We as turkey hunters should not be satisfied until the recognition the great turkey-call makers receive is comparable to that of the artists who produced the finest decoys.

26

THE PURE MEASURE

It is simple to measure success in turkey hunting. The successful hunter is the one who *consistently* kills birds in an ethical manner. There are those who argue that the hunter should only be measured by his respect for the game. That sounds nice, but a lot of wonderful nature lovers don't have the requisite skills, or toughness, to kill turkeys.

All that counts is determination and competence. It does not matter what color your skin is, what school you went to, what clubs you belong to, how many dollars you have in the bank, or if you are generous and kind, or mean and cruel.

There is a parallel with other sports. In the batter's box, all that is relevant is athletic ability and courage. The racists could not keep Henry, Frank, Willie, Joe, or Reggie off the baseball field. Their hands were too quick, their courage too real, their determination too great.

The rednecks could yell their vicious slurs from the darkness of the upper deck, but in the bright glare of the field, the proud black men established themselves as the best. It was the game itself—with its wonderfully pure measure of competence—that selected them. Sinfully inferior educational opportunities could not keep them off the field. Anyone with slightly above-average problem-solving abilities, money, and time can earn a medical degree, law degree, or Ph.D.; only the select few can handle a ninety-four-mile-per-hour fastball.

The pure measure selected not just for athletic ability and courage, but also for intelligence. Henry Aaron and his colleagues outsmarted shrewd pitchers and managers. They were impossible to intimidate. When the pitcher threw at their heads, they picked themselves up and *jumped* on the next pitch. After a while managers learned that they were most dangerous after being knocked down. Gene Mauch, the cerebral manager, fined his pitchers if they threw at Willie or Henry. Mauch knew if you tried to intimidate them, they would beat your club—*by themselves*. Aaron refused to be intimidated even by death threats. When he was closing in on Ruth's lifetime home run record, racists tried to keep him off the diamond by calling in and announcing that they were going to shoot him. The bastards even threatened his kids. His teammates admit *they* were terrified. In America, in 1974, it was not too far out to think that some crazy might try to stop Henry with a rifle. Aaron walked into the illuminated batter's box—the perfect target—and maintained his concentration. He is an American hero. It is a disgrace that the name *Henry Aaron* does not grace the new stadium in Atlanta.

The worst aspects of contemporary sports do not keep the pure nature of the games from thrilling us. Contemporary college basketball is plagued by evils. On most campuses, the concept of the "student-athlete" is a joke. The athletes are essentially professionals who are at college only to play the game. Few are capable of writing grammatically correct English at the *end* of their college careers. Some universities accept the immoral concept that players are not *expected* to graduate. One basketball powerhouse, for example, has not had a single member of its basketball team graduate for the past five years.

The arrogance of some of the coaches is appalling. Listen to them when they argue about the need to do away with the modest academic requirements that make it impossible for some athletes to gain access to their schools. They argue, with fervor, that the kids are the victims of a racist plot that discriminates against the poor black who, for cultural reasons, cannot achieve the needed scores. As long as the kid is six foot six and quick, the coaches' righteous concern is profound. See what concern they show for the small nonathletic black from a disadvantaged background.

As a college teacher, I should probably be immune to the evils of the system. I'm not. The pure measure of the game subverts my outrage. I was captivated by the determination the University of Connecticut brought to the national championship basketball game in 1999. Told they had no chance, counted out by all the experts, they refused to be defeated. They were marvelous. For all the evils of the system, each instant of the forty-minute game was thrilling. The athletes were focused, poised, skilled, and courageous. Their coach led them with intelligence, composure, and creativity. It was the *pure measure* of the game that made the forty minutes magical.

Pursuits other than team sports can also produce the pure measure. The key is that they must be *critical* to participants. When asked why he raced cars, a world-famous driver said, "You do it because it is important to do something difficult well."

For those of us who hunt turkeys, it is the inherent difficulty that makes doing it well important. The difficulty is basic to the pure measure. If the test is pure, you will not be able to buy competence. Many of the greatest hunters have a limited collection of gear. You do not *need* the finest gun; your intelligence, ability, toughness, and determination will determine your success. Put a forty-thousand-dollar Purdey in the hands of a phony and you still have a phony. Put a hundred-dollar Mossberg in the hands of a great turkey hunter and you still have a great turkey hunter.

The pure measure selects for a certain kind of character. If you consistently meet the challenges of hunting wild turkeys, you should be able to get by on talent in other pursuits. The pure measure selects for those who have become proficient by working hard, and these folks tend to be good at anything they deem to be important.

It is difficult to develop confidence when there is no pure measure. If success is based on having to look good or say the right thing to your boss, you must *know* that you are not earning it. Our educational system teaches students that appearance is critical. Go to an undergraduate career day, when the business types come in to recruit. They all look like they came out of a mold—even the colors of their ties will be the same! The poor college kids, desperate for jobs, will also try to look correct. And they, too, will all look alike. Most of them will have been trained to work in the same way. They will be taught to produce what in the Officer Corps of the Army was called a "splashy briefing"— that means "a lot of bullshit." It means charts and graphs that look good, with no need to say anything of substance. The kids will also be taught to gain skill in "networking." Networking is the process by which success is achieved through knowing the right people. Has a great turkey hunter ever achieved his status by networking? Not a chance. I hear people suggest the most important decision you make in terms of future success is which fraternity or sorority to join. Give me a break.

The lack of a pure measure in so many career areas creates tremendous injustices. I have had great students who never were hired for tenure-track teaching jobs because of their candor and honesty. The prospective employers correctly suspected they would not be "yes men." The academic arena does not afford many pure measures of competence. I believe a few of my best students scared some of the people in the departments that did not hire them. The fact they were so bright hurt their chances! A few may have not dressed correctly. Unlike the athlete, the great student did not have the opportunity to say, "Let me go one on one with the other guy you are thinking about hiring." The guys who often get hired are the ones who look good, are glib, and are socially skilled—and are not the ones who can perform when the measure is *pure*.

When the measure is pure, it doesn't matter how you dress. None of the great hunters or anglers I have known would look good in a magazine ad. Turkey hunters in particular are rarely impressive—our bizarre camouflage makes us all look equally silly. Among great fly anglers, too, there is little concern for appearance when the measure of performance is pure. If I took a photograph of the ten best anglers on the Railroad Ranch stretch of the Henry's Fork of the Snake River in Idaho, they would all look shabby. Their clothes are functional; they are not trying to look like anyone. They are comfortable—change that to *proud*—of what they are. As soon as they began to fish, anyone who laughed at their clothes would see their casting stroke and the smile would disappear. Why would they want to look like the guy in a magazine ad? They *know* he couldn't handle the pure measure of the Railroad Ranch.

You can pretend to be one of the great ones. You can dress like they do, use the same gun and calls, but none of that means anything unless you can produce. All the stickers on your car, all the right clothes and equipment mean nothing if you cannot meet the pure measure.

It is interesting how often people with prestigious jobs are captivated by the desire to perform well, and measure up, when the measure is pure. I have seen the most powerful men in this nation watch with awe as great anglers or hunters practiced their special magic. The man might be the top dog in the firm, but he would give *anything* to be able to do what that quiet guy of modest economic means can do with the rod or gun.

There are false measures of skill. We must be cautious about putting too much emphasis on a trophy animal or fish. In theory, an exceptionally large specimen—or one with large antlers, horns, tusks, or spurs—will be a more difficult challenge as a function of the statistical fact that exceptional creatures are rare; moreover, they are usually older, and hence more likely to have acquired skills of predator avoidance. The exceptional specimen is, however, not always a challenge. I recently watched a television program in which a pair of anglers were catching huge trout in a stream in northern Georgia. The situation was artificial. Essentially, the trout were tame and raised to huge size in a stream that had been protected from angling pressure. The challenge was not pure. You can raise a ten-pound trout in an aquarium. The same is true of elk that are raised on ranches. The challenge of killing one is the same as that of killing any domesticated animal. The fact the antlers are huge is irrelevant in the context of the "hunting" accomplishment. It is a false measure.

You might argue that the rich angler who travels to Alaska or New Zealand is also reducing the challenge by his allocation of dollars. I disagree. It is true that the challenge is less on water that has little competition, but that does not obviate the fact that the fish you catch are wild. The quest for the "grand slam" of mountain sheep is comparable. Yes, you must have considerable wealth to pursue the sheep, and that reduces competition; but you still must have the stamina and skill to meet the pure measure of hunting wild creatures in natural settings.

Pure measures are available to Americans. You do not have to have the athletic skills of the great ballplayers or the wealth of the big-game hunter to take on the challenge of consistently killing the American wild turkey. If you succeed, you can be as proud as anyone, anywhere, facing any type of pure measure of competence.

27

THE AMERICAN GAME

One of my most pleasant memories of spring turkey hunting does not involve birds. My Saturday afternoons during turkey season, in a state in which the season has always ended at either 11 A.M. or noon, are spent watching Major League Baseball's *Game of the Week* on television. For me the passive activity provides the perfect balance for the intensity of the hunt.

I normally eat a relaxed lunch with my family and then ask permission to watch the game. It is clearly self-indulgent to spend time in another solitary way. All the members of my nuclear family tease me about my escape onto the couch in the dimly lit gun room, but they enjoy my being able to relax.

The pace of the wonderful game allows you to unwind. Listen to the tone of the great baseball announcers and you will recognize that there is a pervasive calmness in the presentation of the contest. My setting—a dark, quiet room surrounded by mounted turkeys, guns, calls, and prints—contributes to the ambience. The room was built in the basement, and its location confers coolness. I would not consider going out in the glaring sun to watch a game. The dark room allows my tired body and mind to relax and enjoy, in the most passive of ways, a game that is as uniquely American as wild-turkey hunting.

I am not a great fan. I have picked up a lot of the names and some of the records, but I have friends who make me look ignorant. I also never played baseball at a level that would have instilled significant knowledge; still, I love the game's challenges and complexities and marvel at the skills and toughness of the great players. Many of us who have enjoyed success in other games are humble as we watch major-league players consistently get base hits. Reflect on the skills of an Aaron, Mays, Mantle, Ted Williams, or Frank Robinson. Can you imagine hitting more than five hundred home runs at the major league level? And there are current players who are equally skilled who simply have not had time to hit five hundred homers. Today you can watch Sosa, Griffey, McGwire, Bernie Williams, and others who are maintaining high levels of performance. The athletes are just incredible.

The fact that I am not committed to a particular team contributes to the relaxation. Without a favorite team, I find the *Game of the Week* as lacking in passion as wild turkey hunting is passionate. Depending on how late it is in the season, or how enervating the particular morning may have been, my head will begin to nod as fatigue begins to numb my body and mind. It is a "good tired," and I feel no compulsion to fight the numbness. The fatigue has also been acquired honorably. I have worked as hard as possible, and have nothing left. I am comfortable with the commitments I have made to my profession and my family and believe I have earned the right to hunt until I am exhausted. When my head nods, my daughters will tease me about missing the game; in reality, its pace—and frequent replays—allows me to maintain a sense of its flow.

My mind will often wander into the morning or days ahead. The game allows—or even encourages—reflection on other events. Look at the athletes in the dugout. The intensity that is part of the makeup of individuals on other sport teams is not there. You won't see the riveted attention of the players on the hockey bench. The guys who are not on the field are chewing sunflower seeds and joking with one another. There are a lot of hot, long afternoons and you have to pace yourself. When they get into the batter's box, the focus is there, but they learn to relax between the periods of intensity. The baseball season, like the turkey season, is long; it, too, is a kind of marathon.

To succeed in either pursuit, you must accept frequent failures and maintain a calm sense of the need to persevere over the long haul. Have you ever taken a look at the number of games lost by the most successful managers in the history of baseball? The American game teaches you to accommodate failures. In the context of individual performances, the very best of the incredible athletes fail to get a base hit seven times out of ten. Probably the statistic most ingrained in the American sports psyche—even today—is Babe Ruth's sixty-home-run season. The more defining statistic, in the context of understanding the special game, is that the Babe *struck out 1,330 times* during his career.

The accomplished turkey hunter learns to deal with failure. Find a wild-turkey hunter who always succeeds and you have also found a liar or someone who is not hunting in the big leagues; that is, he has either unsophisticated birds, exclusive access to large areas, or unethical hunting techniques.

I celebrate the toughness of the American game as I celebrate the toughness of turkey hunting. Every time I see a European soccer player roll on the ground in apparent agony after a modest collision, I get agitated and wonder how he would perform if he had to stand in against Roger Clemens or some other pitcher who is ready to "come inside"—in other words, throw the ball at his head. The game of baseball selects against a lot of aspiring athletes. I take no small satisfaction in the fact that this game of wild-turkey hunting also selects against phonies. They may try it, or even go through the motions for a couple of days, but they will not persist. Like baseball, it is just too tough for a lot of folks.

28

CARTER'S

Turkey hunters have tracts of hunting land they love. Successful hunting is predicated on access to productive habitat. Most of us develop ties to a few special private tracts. My favorite is Carter's.

The Carter farm is west of the town of Lexington in western Virginia. Three generations of Carters have lived on the tract of approximately eight hundred acres of Big House Mountain for more than fifty years. The mountain farm is wonderful turkey habitat. My home in the town of Lexington is fourteen minutes by vehicle from the property. I have hunted the property since 1978.

The story of the property is not simply that of the wonderful hunting it has provided. My time on the property has afforded an introduction to the history of the area and the subculture of the residents.

The general area was first settled by the Scotch-Irish in the late eighteenth century. The earliest settlers took possession of the most attractive farmland in the rich floodplains along the streams that feed the James River and make up the lower part of the valley. The Carter farm is off the floodplain and qualifies as an "Appalachian Mountain farm," meaning that there is little flat ground and a lot of rock. The farm consists of ridges and hollows with small fields. The earliest European-American inhabitation of what is today the property probably took place in the first two decades of the nineteenth century. There is a rich oral tradition of eighteenth-century occupation and Indian fighting on the Carter property; however, archaeological data speaks to an initial occupation of no earlier than the first decade of the nineteenth century. By that date, the population was no longer concerned about hostile Indians.

The area owned by the Carters was occupied by more people in the nineteenth and early twentieth centuries than are there today. The population was significant from 1825 until 1910. That period spans important episodes in our history. The residents were in their cabins when Lee had his bad day at Gettysburg and Custer had his at the Little Big Horn.

The old homesites are haunting. All that remains are the foundations, artifacts scattered on the ground, and a few domesticated plants that have survived the decades. The artifacts speak to life in the cabins. Pieces of ceramics are evidence of what must have exciting trips to towns and stores. Doll parts are common. They pay testimony to the roles of children and laughter that echoed through the high hollows. On the grim side are the many fragments of medicine bottles. They tell us of attempts to cope with the many diseases the residents faced. We should not forget how different health care was in rural areas in the nineteenth century than it is today. A lot of children died. Infections that would be treated efficiently today killed strong adults who never heard the word *penicillin*. There must have been many endless nights in the cabins when loved ones did not get well.

We found an old photograph of an early cabin on Carter's. It had a scary-looking wooden chimney, and was very small. Posed outside the cabin is an extended family of tough-looking men and women. Most of the adult men were carrying Model 97

Winchester shotguns. I was so impressed with the picture, and the local tradition of the old Model 97s, that I bought one that now hangs next to the guns I use on the property.

I often reflect on the men who hunted the property in the past. I have found old shot-shell cases while hunting. Most of the old shells are Winchesters, and the few on which the shot size is still decipherable indicate that they held the somewhat unusual Number 5s. Many times, while sitting in a blind, I have reflected on who selected the Number 5 shot in an earlier time. I have every confidence he was competent. I enjoy the connection I feel to him.

In addition to historic homesites, the Carter property provides evidence of an earlier history. I have found lithic projectile points that suggest the area was hunted thousands of years ago by Native Americans. These artifacts are often near the sites of the nineteenth-century cabins, because proximity to water sources, flat land, and protection from winds has always attracted humans.

The old roads are also a wonderful artifact of earlier residents. Most that cut through the property were made by loggers. Timbering occurred in stages, for the renewable resource was harvested whenever it achieved marketable size. It would be fascinating to have photographs of the area before the first timbering. It would not have been as good turkey habitat—too many conifers and not enough mast-producing hardwoods. Certainly the ground cover would not have been as dense, and the woods would have been darker.

There is also some evidence of historic fires. Many old stumps carry the scars of fires that occurred less than one hundred years ago. These fires were probably associated with the iron mining industry that was so important in the area for the last half of the nineteenth century. Old iron furnaces can be found less than ten miles from the farm.

The stumps of old chestnut trees are still easy to find. What a magnificent hardwood forest it must have been before the blight took them in the early part of this century. The woods are now predominantly oak, hickory, poplar, and dogwood, with some beech and conifer. Oak is the dominant species; there are white, chestnut, black, and red varieties. The property has particularly good stands of white oaks. In a good mast year there are stands where you cannot take a step without crushing multiple acorns. Wild turkeys killed in the fall of the year will often have craws stretched tight with the large acorns.

The area is also well watered by one good-sized stream, a number of small creeks, and many springs. You are never far from water. The steepness of some of the slopes—some are difficult to stand on—results in areas that are difficult to access. The fact that the eight hundred acres are contiguous to several other large tracts creates a wonderful refuge for turkeys. No maintained roads bisect the property, and most of the logging roads are too rough for anything but walking.

When I began to hunt the property in 1978, the Carter family consisted of Lanny, the widow of the original owner, and her son and his wife. Lanny's husband and another son had both been killed in farming accidents involving the use of tractors on the steep slopes. Lanny was an invalid for most of the years I hunted the property. She died in 1996, and the land is in the process of being divided among heirs. Lanny's son, Donald; his wife, Pattie; and their two children live on the property.

The property does not provide adequate income for the family. As is true of many local farms, its steep slopes and rocks make much of the land marginal for agriculture. The Carters run a few cattle, grow vegetables in a large garden, and cut hay. Supplemental income is produced by cutting firewood and wage earning in Lexington. Donald works for the city. Periodically the family sells some timber off the property to supplement their income. Many local farm families have similar economic situations. For some, the rising value of mountain property for residential building has caused them to sell tracts of their land. The Carters have sold only one small piece.

One of the wonderful aspects of developing a relationship with a piece of property is the intimacy you develop with it. It does more than make for more effective hunting. My partner and I have coined names for many areas of Carter's. One ridge is named for an anonymous, but very loud, dog that disrupted one of our early hunts. Often areas are named for events. There is Heartbreak Ridge where I missed two great gobblers. There is the incredible Adams Ridge, where Jim Adams killed a great nineteen-pound bird on the first day of the 1979 season. In years since, I have called up nine spring gobblers from that precise place. In the Bear Saddle a good-sized black bear almost ran over me while sprinting away from another hunter in the spring of 1987.

I enjoy the fact that sections of the property are remote. The steepness of the slopes and the areas of dense vegetation make it unlikely that many people will make the effort to get into the most isolated areas. In more than a hundred spring hunts, I have encountered only one other hunter at close range—Donald Carter himself. I love the fact that I can get to areas where the only other two-gaited footsteps I hear will be those made by a wild turkey.

There is a network of old logging roads on the property that I know as well as any paved roads in the world. I can walk them in the dark or in dense fog. I have trees I have watched grow over the years. Some of the great oaks have not changed much, but I always enjoy seeing them in the warmth of spring and the cold of winter.

Huge hardwoods have grown around wire fences that were nailed to the trees when they were small. A couple of the trees have strands of barbed wire coming out of the very middle of their two-foot-diameter trunks. In some cases these early fences are in the steepest and most inaccessible sections of the property.

There are small springs high on the mountain where I have never seen another human. I feel comfortable drinking their water, and I have great memories of days when the drinks were part of my private celebration after killing a gobbler. After the celebration, I have had the luxury of relaxing in these remote spots and enjoying them without the distracting intensity of the hunt. There is a calmness I feel when I escape the need to rush back to obligations that so frequently make my time in the field pressured.

An adjoining property was timbered in the 1980s, and the devastation left me ill. The timbering seemed to change the topography. Obviously it did not change the landforms, but it seemed to have, because the trees had been critical in providing a sense of the place. The scars of the clear-cutting are still there a decade later. Trees may be renewable, but no one now living will see the types of white oaks that once grew there.

Investing so many hours on the property means there are few areas that do not hold memories for me. I love to see the trees that I sat up against during past hunts. I often take the time to search for the old shell case that I always leave if I kill a bird. The old cases lose their color with age, but the plastic and metal make for a durable artifact. I never forget spots where I missed a bird or made a terrible decision that deprived me of a chance for a kill. I remember good friends that I have taken to the property over the years. The list includes some who are no longer living.

I love to see evidence of early activities on the property. There are domestic plants still growing at old homesites where there is no longer any evidence of the frail buildings. The only evidence consists of the durable plants.

The property has provided the thrill of black bear and bobcat sightings. The fact that these wild and elusive creatures still live in the area, close to interstates and towns, is a testimony to their adaptability and the inaccessibility of this isolated place.

Knowing an area's topography is a wonderful advantage to hunting efficiency. When I hear a turkey gobble—even at some distance—it is rare that I do not know precisely where he is. Knowing the terrain also allows me to move to birds along the many logging roads and ridgetops that are in my memory.

All the memories are a function of the generosity and trust of the Carters. I do not take it for granted. I have tried to say thanks with the occasional turkey, grouse, or ham at Christmas. These modest tokens are never enough. How much is it worth to be able to hunt eight hundred acres of prime turkey habitat whenever I feel like it? I could not put a price on it. How does the enjoyment I have derived from the property compare to entertainment I have paid for? My last tickets to a Broadway play cost eighty bucks apiece. How does that evening compare to a *season* on Carters?

It is hard to ask people for permission to hunt. It is asking a lot. Not only are you asking the owner to trust you with the dangerous firearm you carry, but every time you hunt you are, to a degree, intruding on his privacy. In some cases the property owners, or members of their families, are hunters as well, and if they grant you permission to hunt they are introducing competition that has the potential to reduce their chances for success. The Carters have been exceedingly generous with their property. I do not have to call before I hunt, and I can make the decision to go at the last minute.

Some people decline my requests to hunt even after I have done favors for them or members of their families. I have never done more for the Carters than make small gifts at Christmas. When I thank Donald, it always gives me a lift to hear him say, "Sure, you come back *anytime.*"

29

NATIVE SONS

I like Americans. My career in anthropology has taken me from the jungles of Peru to the Outer Hebrides of Scotland and the outback of Australia. Studying other cultures has convinced me that Americans look good by comparison.

I remember watching an American astronaut on the deck of a huge aircraft carrier after they picked him out of the Pacific. I don't remember his name or the name of his ship, but I do remember what he said to the crew: "I understand you guys missed a weekend leave to pick us up. I am *really sorry* our schedule screwed you up." A lifetime of travel and a couple of years in the military gave me a pretty good idea of how a hero in the uniform of any other nation would have responded. He would not have given a shit about his supporting cast. The American astronaut, in his moment of glory, did not see himself as superior to the guys on the deck. To me, at that instant, he was the quintessential native son.

Another native son showed me the special American trait of self-confidence in the company of others who have enjoyed greater advantages. Ted Corrigan was from Bucks County, Pennsylvania. The time period was the 1950s, and the remarkably beautiful area had not yet been impacted by insane population growth. Many successful men selected Bucks County as the perfect place to live as they worked on the fastest of fast tracks in "The City." They would return from New York to relax on one of the perfect Bucks County farms. Ted was one of the few natives of what was, in his youth, the country town of New Hope, Pennsylvania. He painted my parents' home. He and my father would talk for hours about their experiences in the Pacific Theater of World War II. They talked as equals because they perceived themselves as such. Try to find that kind of relationship between the successful man in Europe or Asia and anyone who works for him. This confident, intelligent, proud, and capable man became a good friend of my parents, and they celebrated the fact he was my first hunting mentor. I learned a lot more than hunting skills from Ted, and my parents saw the exposure as an important part of my education.

When I reflected on Ted upon hearing of his death, the picture I had was of him eating lunch with my parents at the big table in the kitchen of the Bucks County farmhouse. My father, mother, and Ted would laugh about Prohibition, sing the praises of FDR, and cry about the friends they lost on the *Arizona* or the Burma Trail. I remember one clear realization that came to me as I listened to the three kind, tough, capable, unassuming, and decent native "sons" at their long lunches: The ruthless Japanese never had a chance.

When I was a kid, my heroes were a couple of outdoor writers who were native sons. Their names were Trueblood and McClane. They were honest and informative and used simple yet precise language. They displayed no macho bravado or locker room crudeness. Experiences with their wives, rather than girlfriends, were woven into their articles. They had a quiet confidence that was the product of having done what they talked about. They highlighted errors they made and laughed at them.

But the clear competence was apparent. They had the purest kind of confidence: They had nothing to prove. When you tried something they suggested, it worked. One was a westerner, the other from the East, but the common denominator was that they were native sons. They were great ambassadors of this nation. They had that uniquely American trait of being ready to meet anyone, king or guide, as an equal.

Some native sons had parents who came from the Old Country. One was a gunsmith, in the Old World sense of a man who has been an apprentice and achieved the status of craftsman. As is the case with many native sons, his progress had not been easy. He dropped out of school to help his German-speaking farm family make it through the depression. I was a kid when I met him in his small but elegant gun shop. He built the business by being fair and good at what he did. He was patient and informative with young boys who were obsessed with guns and hunting. He taught us as well as served us. His shop had items from Germany—glass, clothes, and silver—and a collection of the fine commercial guns of the 1960s. He made custom hunting rifles. Most were built on Pre 1964 Model 70 Winchester actions. He did *all* the wood- and metalwork himself.

His shop was a refuge for those who loved wonderful outdoor tools. He had Pendleton wools, Stetson hats, and Burberry coats *before* they became the in things to wear. Many of his customers were well educated and affluent, and he learned from them because he was intelligent and listened. He had never had a course in economics, but he learned about Wall Street and made sound investments. As other hardworking native sons have done, he became a financial success. In the 1960s he sold more high-grade Browning Superposed guns than anyone on the East Coast. He developed a loyal clientele. He took no shortcuts. He cheated no one.

He was extraordinarily generous. When I finally was able to afford a Browning Superposed, he reached for one of the handsome cases and said, with a warm wink, "It comes with one of these." An Italian-American lady named Angela who worked for him was having trouble with her car. I knew it was one of the many problems in her life. He bought her a vehicle. His kindness and generosity paid dividends. When gun shops began to be targeted by burglars in the 1960s, he worried about his level of liability, and I heard him ask several of his regular customers for advice. The word must have gotten out that George was asking about insurance. One day a limo stopped in front of the shop, and several well-dressed Italian-Americans got out. George said they looked like "successful businessmen." Only one talked, and he said, "You were very kind to buy Angela a car." George acknowledged that he had made the gift. The spokesman for the group continued, "We understand you are worried about the possibility of your shop being burglarized." Confused, George said, "Yes, I am." The well-dressed man responded, "We are here to tell you that will never happen—*ever*." Geoge said the man shook his hand, walked out of the store, and he never saw any of them again. At the time some gun stores in Trenton, New Jersey, were hit more than once a month. In the subsequent thirty-four years there never was an attempt on George Schielke's shop.

The remarkable record the native sons established in standing against the most frightening tyrants is explicable. The historians called them "citizen-soldiers" and marveled at what they accomplished against the immaculate German professionals. The reason was that the nation had made them tough and creative. Hitler's boys seemed invincible until units got split up in the desert, or on the tundra, or in the towns. Their subordinates were not trained to take command. They were taught to do their own jobs well, and as long as the structure was in place, they functioned with frightening effectiveness. The difference is that when the captain from West Point went down, a native son— some bright kid off the farm, or from one of the countless small towns or huge cities—stepped forward because he had been taught to feel no inferiority. The group did not miss a beat, and soon the members of the Wehrmacht unit had their collective hands in the air as the native son, probably not dressed in the most impressive uniform, made it very clear that the Germans' visions of invincibility needed reassessment.

When the Japanese dove their kamikaze aircraft at our ships and committed suicide in the name of their emperor, the kid from Kansas did not fold. His toughness was a legacy of his grandparents, who had met the challenges of the prairie. He stood by the gun, protecting his buddies, and he won the war in the Pacific.

These native sons were the same characters who became legendary hunters. They were not great hunters by birth; they became great by taking advantage of the opportunities the democratic land provided. In many cases native sons were not given the chance to achieve advanced degrees, or careers in medicine, law, or other professions, but they were not deprived of the opportunity to become the best turkey hunters in their county. A capable young man from a poor family in England, on the other hand, would never be given a chance to show how he could perform on driven grouse. That was the domain of the rich or those born to high status.

I speak of native *sons* here because the subculture of turkey hunting remains essentially male, but there is no doubt that the success of women in working toward equality in this nation is part of the same story. It was not just the kid from Kansas who won the war in the Pacific. There were the anonymous American women who built the ships that took the fight to the Imperial Japanese Navy. The women worked long hours for low wages in the shipyards. One was Lucille Gewitz of New York. She graduated from Hunter College in 1942, and she worked with countless other women for ship maker CIO. They built the great battleship the *Missouri* by working for fifty-three cents an hour. I saw a picture of Ms. Gewirtz and her female colleagues at the South Street Seaport Museum in New York. She and her friends are dressed in overalls. They look proud, strong, and competent, and they are all smiling great American smiles. They look invincible. I would have loved to have seen them, wherever they were, when MacArthur dictated the terms of the surrender to the Japanese officials on the deck of the *Missouri*. Ms. Gewitz and the other women built that ship. Can you imagine the pride the women must have felt as watched their American brothers end the war the Japanese thought they had won at Pearl Harbor?

Those women refused to accept the idea that they did not have the inherent skills of men, and in the land of the brave they changed the rules against the most difficult of odds. Amelia Earhart, the gentle, demure woman who knew no fear, may have been the bravest of our native "sons." American women were destined to lead the movement to escape inequity and get closer to equality. Despite what the culture of the military and the corporations say, they may be our toughest native "sons."

The story does not apply solely to hunters. Every time someone tells me that the best anglers in the world are rich men in England who buy access to private chalk streams, I reflect on the native sons who fish the great *public* waters of this nation. These waters are available to anyone who is good enough. It will cost you nothing to fish Silver Creek or the Henry's Fork, but you had better come ready to compete with the best anglers in the world. These native sons are the best because there is no restriction on the competition. There is no daily rod fee, and many of the very best anglers are of modest economic means. The reason the Itchen, the Test, or any stream in New Zealand cannot be the best challenge is because only the wealthy will be there. The photograph of the huge brown trout you took from the remote New Zealand river will not impress me. The helicopter, the talented guide, the dollars, and the lack of competition are the reasons why you hold the fish.

If you want to find out how good you are, come to the accessible Railroad Ranch of the Henry's Fork and try to catch the fish that have been educated by native sons named Harrop, Traversio, Lawson, Mate, Laughlin, Ishyama, Smith, and Schultz. If you come, you can leave your curriculum vitae at home. If you expect to have success, bring confidence, skill, stamina, and no excuses.

The native sons have the look of the unconquered. Give me a great turkey hunter and I will show you a guy who does not kiss ass. He will not always say the most appropriate thing or wear the correct clothes. He will not be deemed wise. He will not be the most popular attorney in the firm. Why? Because he will call the cheater a cheater. He will be ridiculed as outspoken. At an earlier time these unvanquished men and women took some of the tough stands that allowed the nation to become great. Today they are rare. Corporations and institutions have beaten them into submission. Even tenure doesn't cure cowardice. With tenure, professors have nothing to fear; the problem is that they have forgotten how to be brave.

Thankfully, there remain native sons who will not be intimidated. I think of two outspoken ones who took a stand when they felt that a river they loved was being threatened. When a glib forest service administrator finished telling us why there was no reason for concern about the state of the river, Rick Lawson stood up, faced the administrator, and said *everything* the guy had just declared was bullshit. The target of Rene Harrop's attack was another forest service type who was not ready to meet Rene, Brad Smith, and me when we arrived at the scheduled time. When the guy arrogantly showed up late, Brad and I had to restrain Rene. Some may say it is coincidental that the Henry's Fork has enjoyed greater protection than most other rivers, but I submit that it is not; it is because the river is considered *sacred* by its native sons, and they are ready to fight to protect it.

30

IN DEFENSE OF THE WILD TURKEY

My friend James told me *never* to let anyone be disrespectful to the wild turkey. It was one of the first lessons he taught me, "you have to stand your ground to protect the birds," he said. When trying to protect their status, he has, at times, become pugnacious.

We were sitting around a campfire in a deep West Virginia hollow. The young state game biologist was making an argument about the relative difficulty of hunting trophy deer and mature gobblers. He was arguing the merits of deer. I sat looking down into the hypnotic embers and had an idea what was about to transpire. James sat on his haunches across from the game biologist, staring into the flames. As he stared, he poked a small stick into the fire. The more the game biologist talked, the more James manipulated the stick. I listened to the biologist:

"Now, James, you have to admit that some of those gobblers will do stupid things. Why, old man Conley said some kid bought one of those four-dollar calls and killed a twenty-pounder the next day! Come on, you have to admit they are capable of stupid behavior."

James did not say a word. I wished I were elsewhere.

"I've got you on that one," said the game biologist, sensing he had made a good point. "James, you have to admit I'm right."

James looked back to the fire and then, with the most decisive of motions, drove the small stick into the coals. The sparks flew up and I involuntarily recoiled. James stared intently at the young biologist and said, very slowly, as if explaining something to a child: "The wild turkey gobbler is the king of these mountains. He always has been, and he always will be. Anybody who suggests otherwise is a damned fool."

Now I stared into what was left of the fire to avoid looking at either man. The young biologist laughed and said, "Well, I guess there is no sense in debating with you. You refuse to listen to common sense. Even John will admit a trophy buck is a great creature, right, John?" Wishing I could disappear, I just gazed into the fire. James got me off the hook by standing up, looking off at a distant ridge, and saying, "Six years in college and he argues that a whitetail buck is better game than a mature gobbler. Education is wonderful." Then, without another word, James walked down to his truck.

On another occasion, I was with him when we encountered another hunter at a check-in station. The man was with three friends, and they were in the process of checking in an immature gobbler. The hunter who had killed the bird threw it out of the bed of a pickup truck, looked at us, and said, "See, I told you boys that gobbler could still fly." The young gobbler fell in a heap next to the gas pumps. One of the man's friends followed his lead and picked the bird up and tossed it in the air. Several more raucous remarks were made for the benefit of James, me, and two teenage girls, who smiled coyly at the drama. The man in the back of the pickup, in an effort to solicit a response from James and me, said, "Hey fellows, feel free to shoot that bird if he flies again." James turned to go inside the store, and I followed, feeling very uncomfortable.

The proprietor said hello to me and greeted James in the deferential manner accorded to great turkey hunters in small towns in the American South. James asked if he could check in a gobbler, and I noticed that his voice sounded strained. The proprietor was quick to say he would check the bird, and we went back out to get it. The four men were still involved in the skit with the young gobbler. The audience had been augmented by a husband and wife who laughed loudly at every line. James walked directly to our vehicle and took the gobbler from the backseat. When I saw his face, I knew we would be lucky to leave the store without incident. The man in the back of the pickup saw our bird and half yelled, "Lord have mercy, now *there* is a gobbler!" James didn't look his way. The man added, "Well, boys, there is a man with a real gobbler." I sensed from the tone of his voice he would be willing to let James take center stage. James stopped and looked at the man in the truck. I could not see James's face or eyes, but the man by the pumps stopped tossing the turkey, and the man in the truck stopped talking. James turned quickly and walked into the store.

James checked in the bird. We thanked the proprietor and provided a few polite but brief answers to the inevitable questions about the status of the local turkey population. He then bought a Dr Pepper, asked me if I wanted one, turned, and carried the bird out of the building. The four men were standing by the entrance. As we passed, one said, "That is a great gobbler you have killed, sir." James turned and looked up at the young man, who towered over him. "Your bird is also a beautiful creature, and you should be ashamed of the way you treated it," James replied in a strained voice. "If you ever want to be considered a turkey hunter, the first thing you will have to do is learn to respect these great creatures." The young man muttered, "Yes, sir, we were just acting silly. We didn't mean any disrespect."

It wasn't over. The gentlest man I've ever met—the only person outside the family whom my elder daughter was able to relax with when she was going through her first rough encounter in school—jerked his body up until his eyes were close to the man's face and shouted, "You God-damned idiot! You didn't mean any disrespect when you threw the bird in the dirt? Are you *that* stupid and common? And you," he went on, spinning with athletic quickness toward the three accomplices, "you didn't mean any disrespect when you tossed the gobbler up in the air? I'd like to see *you* tossed in the air and dragged through the dirt."

All three men just stared at their feet. James stood there as the four tough-looking young men muttered apologies. They did not turn as we walked to our vehicle and drove off. I didn't say a word and felt very uncomfortable as we made the trip back into town. Finally, two blocks from my home, James said, "Sorry for that display, John, but don't ever let the rednecks get away with desecrating a gobbler." I smiled and said something about the fact I hoped he hadn't expected me to pull a revolver if they attacked us. He grinned, too, and said, "Not a chance, John—the bigmouths have hearts of jelly." As he said it, the blue eyes were twinkling again.

31

THE TRAP

I believe the greatest satisfaction we derive from turkey hunting comes from doing it well. No one enjoys hunting poorly. If accomplishment is critical, and if the quarry is the wild turkey, there will be frustrations. A series of frustrations can stimulate a sense that you *have* to kill one.

In the spring of 1982 I had finally achieved a level of competence that made me a threat to mature gobblers. I had a wonderful group of productive properties on which to hunt—the key to *intelligent* optimism—and I looked forward to the year with great confidence. I *expected* to kill a bird the first day. After the first *eight* days, though, I had nothing to show for my investment but fatigue, depression about my failure, and a growing spirit of competitiveness with my friends who had enjoyed success. The need to kill a turkey began to haunt me. Each evening it seemed that yet another hunter would call me with a story of a successful hunt. I recognized that my "congratulations" were beginning to sound hollow.

I fell into the terrible trap of allowing the killing of a bird to become too important. Even as I planned my hunt for the ninth morning, I realized I was on the edge. I began to get desperate about selecting the best place to hunt and worried about who might be there, or if one of my successful friends had already killed the bird that had been there before the season. I needed a day of rest, but even with a forecast of bad weather I did not consider not going. I could not afford a rest.

In the morning my head hurt from the fatigue. After washing my face in the sink, the pain remained; I carried it to the field with me. The climb was an ordeal, not the usual invigorating exercise. As I sat against a tree, waiting for dawn, there was a general dullness to my cognition.

The gobble brought a measure of excitement back, but I felt the indecision that accompanies a lack of confidence. I finally decided to go after the bird. As I got close to him, I stopped and listened for other hunters. Two days before a hunter had cut me off from a bird, and I worried about a recurrence of that incident. This time there were no other hunters in the area. Still, listening to the bird gobble was not as enjoyable as it usually was. I was too desperate to kill him.

The decision to begin calling came quickly. The bird responded well and my excitement grew. When the bird began to make his way up the ridge, I could feel the tension grow. I *had* to convert this opportunity. Instead of the wonderful anticipation, the fear of missing began to run through my brain. As the gobbler came to the edge of shotgun range, my tension became intense. I moved the barrel slightly and immediately realized that my movement had been too quick. The bird jerked his head up to full height. "Too far?" The question was critical, but I did not respond quickly enough. My hesitation was all the bird needed. He wheeled around and was gone. My incredibly awkward attempt to stand provided me with the disheartening view of a turkey getting farther and farther out of shotgun range. I felt my heart beating rapidly with the trauma of the failure. I was ready to cry. The depression was profound. The great opportunity had been squandered. The day was young, but I *knew* there would be no other chance.

A cumulative sense of failure overwhelmed me. I sat down and began to wonder if it would ever end. The terrible thought that I was destined to failure played on my mind. I admit that I did not want to have to live with that feeling for a full year.

I went through the motions for the rest of the day. I was still turkey hunting, but I had nothing left. When I arrived home, Nell greeted me with, "Do we have a turkey?" It was hard to smile at the question that had so frequently introduced celebration. When she told me Gary had killed another one, I could tell from her expression that she knew it would hurt. I normally celebrated Gary's successes. On this day the news left me speechless. I was not a good companion, or father, for the rest of the weekend.

I looked forward to the following week with resignation rather than anticipation. I tried to rest, but there was too much fatigue and too little time. Hunting became an ordeal as I pressed, made terrible decisions, and discovered new ways to sabotage potentially productive situations.

The final step was when I realized I had lost hope. The last week of the season was a nightmare. I had convinced myself I was not going to kill a gobbler. I went as a function of a need not to quit. The overwhelming sense of failure was frightening. It was as if I were the victim of some kind of black magic. Was some other hunter casting a spell? The idea was ludicrous, but the level of fatigue I was experiencing was having an effect on my mind. I couldn't be this unlucky unless something was contributing to the situation.

This will not be an inspiring story of redemption, or of finding perspective in the last days of the season. There was no turnaround, no final success to erase the disappointment and make the ordeal a lesson in character building. I am sure it was fatigue that resulted in my picking up the flu. Now I had trouble sleeping, and the combination of the fatigue and the illness left me a wreck. My condition deteriorated, and I hunted in a fog. It was not intelligent to be hunting, but I did not want to quit. I made stupid mistakes in the field and finally had a humiliating experience that convinced me I didn't deserve to be hunting.

I had chased one gobbler for most of the morning and, at 10 A.M., set up on a ridge to call to him. Half an hour of calling brought no response, and fatigue had me drifting to sleep. Suddenly I heard an incredible thrashing combined with aggressive purring just off the contour. I knew two birds were fighting almost within range. The thrill of this possible opportunity, after all my frustrations, had me shaking with anticipation as the raucous sounds came closer. I saw the two huge gobblers, with their necks entwined, when they crested the ridge some forty-five yards above me. I wanted a bird badly, but I knew a shot risked the illegal act of killing both turkeys. It was not a good time for ethical considerations. I looked down the rib of the gun at the two birds. For once, they were oblivious to my presence. My confused mind struggled with the situation until I felt the gun jump with the recoil of a shot. *Both* birds flushed and flew through the hardwood cover. I was shaken and humiliated by the experience. Had I pulled the gun away from the birds at the last second? I have no recollection of doing so. It was not a difficult shot, as the birds were relatively stationary and completely consumed by their fight. I think, thankfully, that I had just missed after making the unethical decision to shoot. As I made the difficult walk out of the woods, I engaged in the most critical self-evaluation imaginable.

To maintain an intelligent perspective you must convince yourself that the killing of a turkey is not necessary. It is a balancing act: On the one hand, the pride you derive from doing it well is based on killing birds consistently; however, if the killing becomes too important, you will fall into a terrible trap that can turn the most enjoyable pursuit into a nightmare.

32

MARATHON

Turkey hunting is a marathon. Be it fall or spring, if you do it the way it should be done, it will test your stamina. Beginners make the mistake of thinking it is critical to succeed quickly. This rush for success erodes you physically and emotionally. I know: I was one of those so desperate to get my turkey I never took a break. In the early years I hunted as if I were sprinting. The idea of taking a day off was unthinkable. By the last week of the season, particularly in the spring, I was no longer capable of effective hunting. Exhaustion left me incapable of intelligent decisions. I worked hard to achieve good physical condition before the season, but no regimen of training allows the human body to accommodate weeks of 3:30 A.M. alarms.

I learned that to be effective you must prepare yourself for a marathon. Like a distance runner, you must pace yourself. It is very hard not to go when the weather is good and you haven't killed a bird, but if you do not take a break the last phase of the season will be a disaster. You will make stupid decisions, you will hunt poorly, and the fatigue will make you susceptible to health problems.

Not only must you take days off, but you also have to give yourself a rest when you are not hunting. That is not easy to do with the occupational and family responsibilities most of us have. You will be using all of your free time to hunt, and every other waking moment will be consumed by your job or your family. Guilt can convince you to try to do things that will push you over the edge. One of my worst days *ever* involved an attempt to Christmas shop after four days of fall old gobbler hunting. To say I was not providing quality time for my wife and daughters on that terrible day is a gross understatement.

You must prepare for the marathon not just physically, but also psychologically. One of the factors that discourages many aspiring spring hunters is the frustration some experience early in the spring when the hens have not yet left the gobblers. You should not *expect* to do well at these times, and you cannot afford to burn yourself out before the opportunities improve. The key is to stay ready, and relatively rested, for primetime. Many hunters do not appreciate the fact that the best hunting may come well into the season; by then they will have become so exhausted they are just going through the motions.

It is fascinating to me to see those who are selected against by the marathonlike quality of turkey hunting. They offer creative excuses, including: "Deer hunting is more challenging"; "Fall turkeys are too easy"; "I don't like the taste of spring birds." The explanation I never hear is that the hunting is too tough and the physical demands too great. In reality, the marathon is too much for them.

For one index of the stress imposed by turkey season, just take a look at hunters at the end of either fall or spring. If they are part of the subculture, they will show their exhaustion. One friend of mine looked so terrible that I actually took photographs of him at the end of one spring. Jerry had been trapped by shift work that had him on the job from three to eleven. He essentially was trying to hunt on a couple of hours' sleep a day. When I took his photo, he was a wreck. He might have been a little heavier than they were, but he didn't look much better than the poor Germans who survived Stalingrad.

The glaring contrast between the physical demands imposed by turkey hunting and those of other types makes turkey hunting special. I love to hunt squirrels with a rifle, for instance. The pace is relaxed, and you do not have to cover any ground. You can drive to a nice woodlot, walk a hundred yards, and have a wonderful afternoon sitting up against a tree burning fewer calories than you would mowing the lawn.

A lot of guided waterfowl hunts can be easy, too. If you are carried to a blind in a boat, the only exercise you may get is standing up to shoot and getting back in the boat to return to the lodge. Oh, I grant that the early mornings and cold may help you sleep well, but compare the demands of such a hunt to the experience my partner and I had on the first day of the 1998 fall season. On that arduous day we each walked over twelve miles and climbed almost fifteen hundred feet, carrying thirty pounds of gear and clothing apiece. We took our first step from the car at four forty-five in the morning and returned to it at six-fifteen in the evening. That day was the start of *six weeks* of fall hunting. We took days off from hunting during the six weeks, but not many. At the end of the period we felt as if we had been running an endless marathon. Eating like adolescents, and despite our middle-age metabolisms, we typically lose eight to ten pounds each fall.

I have friends whose favorite hunting is for doves. I enjoy shooting doves, but it is not "hunting." It is a shoot. It takes place in the afternoon; usually you can put in a full day of work beforehand and even act like a human being at a social event that evening. It is casual, relaxed, and easy. Dove shooting is to turkey hunting as playing Frisbee is to Olympic freestyle wrestling.

Yes, there are other forms of hunting that impose marathon-like demands. I cannot afford to hunt sheep, for example, but I am willing to concede that it would likely impose stress comparable to that of turkey hunting. You may cite other forms of hunting as matching the demands of wild-turkey hunting; I accept that. I will not accept that any form of hunting is *more* of a marathon.

I have often thought that determination is the most important factor in a hunter's success. A marathon selects for those who have the stamina and determination to stay the course. The same qualities select for the most successful turkey hunters.

33

TERROR

I approached the familiar ridge with anticipation. It was late in the morning of the final Friday of the spring season. My late start was intentional: I was convinced that this educated gobbler would no longer respond to calls at first light.

My strategy was to make a series of low-volume calls to imitate a relaxed hen enjoying the warmth of the sun and reflecting on activities other than predator avoidance. I was sure the gobbler would not gobble; however, the still morning, the leaf cover on the forest floor, and his gait would allow me to hear him approach as he climbed out of the hollow. The sharp contour of the ridge would prevent him from seeing me until he was within range.

Despite the odds against late-season kills, I enjoyed the confidence of two previous successes, using the same strategy, from precisely the same location. I was not worried about human interference, as it had taken me fifty-five minutes of hard climbing to reach this spot; in addition, in ten seasons I had *never* encountered another hunter on the remote ridge.

I called every fifteen minutes, making only soft purrs and clucks. As always, I enjoyed the sounds of the call, the beauty of the woods, and the excitement of knowing the gobbler was listening. He might take an hour to arrive, but it was easy to be patient.

I heard the characteristic sounds after thirty minutes. The rhythm was that of a two-legged creature, with an occasional pause as the bird hesitated in his characteristically cautious approach. My excitement began to build.

"Stay poised!" I thought. My shaking hands and arms, pounding heart, and rapid breathing were evidence of my lack of control over my nervous system. To say I was excited is an inadequate description of my physiological transformation.

The level of excitement never ceases to amaze me. I had taken a gobbler in the first week of the season, but killing *this* bird was critical. You may try to convince yourself a kill is not important—you will not convince your nervous system.

I tried desperately to stay calm so I could act quickly and efficiently when the gobbler crested the ridge. As always, the sounds of his footsteps were soon so loud it seemed impossible that he was not visible. Suddenly, there was a flash of black on the edge of the ridge.

My brain does not provide adequate recall of the decision-making processes of the next terrifying instant. The identification of the "flash of black" as the top of a camouflage cap *on a human head* left me too weak to stand or speak.

Even with thirty-five years of experience I had allowed my excitement and circumstantial evidence to convince me that a gobbler was coming to my call. For some time, I tried to tell myself it was my need to achieve an absolute identification of the "bird" that allowed me to avoid the accident. That sounded good, but I know I was lucky. Terror still runs through me each time I reflect on the incident—which took place nineteen years ago.

The story indicates how quickly a dangerous situation can arise while turkey hunting. The lesson of my near-tragic error is: *Never assume* that a sound indicates the presence of a wild turkey. The only evidence you can afford to use in determining whether a turkey is coming to your call is seeing the bird *clearly*. Have the discipline to believe that any sound, no matter how realistic and convincing, could be produced by a human. Be *very careful* out there!

34

THE PASSION

Great turkey hunters are passionate. You can sense their passion when you listen to them describe a hunting experience. There will be fire in their eyes and a special pitch to their voices.

You can feel the passion when you hunt with the great ones. There is an intensity, an electric quality to their pursuit. Their bodies are taut with the excitement. *Intensity* may be as close as our language allows us to describe it, but I suspect that hunting cultures had words even more descriptive. During the most critical stages of the hunt—for example, when the bird is coming to your call—the passionate hunter has difficulty because of the impact of the thrill on his physiology: Suber begins to hyperventilate; Adams thinks he is having a heart attack; Franke grips the gun so tightly his hands begin to cramp; Rodgers begins to shake; Fleenor gets violently ill right after the kill. All are manifestations of the passion.

What makes this passion so intense? What sustains it? The great bird is critical. The remarkable creature, this huge bird capable of such incredible physical feats, captivates us. He possesses the quintessential collection of qualities that make a creature "game." As your knowledge of the bird increases, you develop limitless respect for his wariness, toughness, adaptability, courage, and keen eyesight and hearing.

The profound challenges are important. It is a lesson of the human experience that the more difficult the task, the more satisfying its accomplishment. For mountain climbers it is Everest that evokes the greatest passion; for anglers it is the Atlantic salmon and the permit; for hunters it is the desert sheep, kudu, and American wild turkey.

The fact that calling is the method of hunting is relevant. Calling any wild creature is exciting; however, when a *huge* bird materializes from the hardwoods, it will leave you weak with the thrill. In addition, the turkey you successfully call will always be *close*. The intimacy of these encounters contributes to the passion. The calling also feeds the passion by demanding you play an active role. You are so involved.

The anticipation of the hunt feeds the passion. It is so exciting to plan hunts. I remember driving home after a day in the field and seeing an area I had not yet hunted. The thought that I might have the opportunity to go there sent a thrill through me.

Hunters themselves help generate the passion by attributing great importance to the hunt. As we achieve a measure of competence, the incentive to become better grows. In a sense we find ourselves happily consumed by developing our skills. The pursuit of competence—the preparation, practicing, and planning—feeds the passion.

The passion is built by the immense responsibility of killing efficiently. You love the birds and are desperate to kill them cleanly. You are not relaxed when you prepare to kill a wild turkey. As the opportunity for the shot approaches, the pressure is incredible, and that makes even an easy shot difficult. To perform well, you must bring skill, poise, and, yes, passion.

The passion can be sustained by identifying with turkey hunters from the past. It is a subculture with historical depth. A retrospective camaraderie is formed with all those who have been captivated by this pursuit. Old photographs and stories create bonds. It is easy to feel the passion of the early hunters when you see their faces. This heritage contributes to the passion.

I believe the passion is in part atavistic. The hominid nervous system evolved to release adrenaline when a hunt was critical to survival. The killing of a turkey may no longer determine whether you live or die, but there is no way to explain that to your nervous system. Our move away from a hunting-based existence has been too recent for this biological effect to be lost. Think about how staggering the impact of failing to kill a turkey can be. There is no rational reason for it to be so important. It has nothing to do with the economic well-being of your family, there is no public humiliation, there will be another chance. Why, then, does the failure generate such profound depression? Our nervous systems still see the loss of game as catastrophic.

The anxiety generated by the anticipation of killing a game creature—call it buck fever, if you will—is also atavistic. The passionate hunter can be so impacted by the presence of a wild turkey that he will have trouble breathing normally. The racing of your heart, the hyperventilation, and the tremors are all testimony to how important you *believe* the killing of the bird is.

I tell a story to my students in making the atavistic argument: My partner came to my office one spring morning lamenting what he described as the loss of a turkey. He said, "Another disaster, I missed another one!" I am one of the more gullible people around, but in this case I knew Gary was trying to deceive me. It was not that his acting was so terrible, but rather that he could not keep his eyes from gleaming with the thrill of having killed one. He could feign an expression of grief, but his nervous system would not go along with his conscious attempt to deceive. I believe what ignited the spark in his eyes was a nerve, or nerves, that still functions the way it did in our prehistoric past.

Are all humans susceptible to becoming passionate about the hunt? My experiences, and instincts, tell me the answer is no. I would go farther and suggest that the passion is less likely to be found in females than in males. I know women who are passionate hunters, but they are rare. I believe the reason is that most cultures have conditioned females to pursue interests other than hunting. And I would add that this direction has given women other domains that allow for the development of passion. It is fascinating to see the different cultural circumstances that produce passionate hunters. It is understandable in groups in which hunting is economically important, or highly respected, but I often wonder how it can skip generations in a culture that has been removed from hunting. Many of us know young boys who grew up in urban areas with parents who had no interest in hunting—yet the passion emerged in them.

Is it possible that the tedious and unrewarding nature of many contemporary jobs explains why hunting can become such a passion? Some occupations offer satisfaction and enjoyment, but few generate passion. I do not think it is coincidental that some of the most passionate hunters I know have jobs that afford little pride, satisfaction, or fulfillment. Two good friends, and great turkey hunters, work in mills at jobs that are tedious and limiting. Hunting has become their passion.

Historians have argued that hunting would not have generated such passion for warriors of the plains, who lived lives of constant challenges and thrills. I don't buy it. I suspect that the great warrior—he who was respected as the bravest of the brave—still trembled with the thrill of the hunt.

To be competent, you have to find, nurture, and maintain the passion. Without it you have no chance of success—be it while trying to conquer the great mountain, fool the wily fish, or kill the mature gobbler.

35

THE IMPORTANCE OF TURKEY CALLS

The lady at the bank was upset. "I am not sure I understand, Dr. McDaniel. You want to put *turkey calls* in your safe deposit box?" Before I could answer, she continued, "If this is some kind of practical joke that you and your students are involved with, I do not find it very amusing." She stared at the shopping bag I was carrying. I opened it and pulled out the carefully wrapped calls. I said, "It's not a joke. They are *very* valuable." She stared at me for several seconds, then said, "Well, I guess there is no rule against putting turkey calls in our vault if you want to pay for the space."

Each June, after our spring season, I go to my local bank and put my calls in the box along with my wills, stocks, bonds, deeds, car titles, and birth certificates. The second year I arrived with the calls, the president of the bank appeared. He eased into the vault and gave me his small-town banker's smile. As I put the calls in the box, he kept looking out the door as if he expected an accomplice to come in with a tommy gun. I asked him if he had ever hunted turkeys. He said, "No," and it was clear from his tone that he did not think hunting turkeys was very important.

After I closed the box, I could not resist telling him: "You should try investing in some turkey calls instead of those junk bonds you keep buying. In thirty years my daughters will be able to sell the calls I just put in that box and pay for my grand-child's law-school education at Stanford."

He tried to give me the "smile" but my comment must have short-circuited some nerve endings. His face twitched, and the shape of his mouth wasn't correct as he moved to the side to let me out of the vault. I walked out of the building in which he was trapped.

Not all turkey hunters keep their calls in banks, but all of us will agree they are *important*. I would argue that no form of hunting places more importance on calling.

There is a tradition of calling in waterfowl hunting, but few hunters with experience in both pursuits would make a case for the waterfowl call being as critical to success. Effective waterfowl hunting involves selecting a place ducks and geese are using and putting out decoys for them to see. If you are in the right place, you don't have to make a single call; moreover, if a guy is in the wrong place, he can blow a call all day long and never attract a duck.

The call is crucial to virtually all ethical turkey hunting. You've probably read stories that suggest woods skills are more important than calling. And it's true that some accomplished hunters are not great callers. In today's competitive environment, however, they are the exception rather than the rule. I am not saying that you have to have contest-level skills—just that the best turkey hunters are skilled callers, period.

One of the great appeals of calling is that it demands you play an active role. In addition, it is more satisfying to convince birds to come to you than to simply walk them up. Anyone who has had the opportunity to hunt ducks by both calling them and jumping them will agree that the calling strategy is more satisfying. My partner and I have jumped our share of mallards off small streams and ponds. The technique requires hard work, and it is certainly ethical—you could even argue that the shooting is more difficult than when you call the birds to you. Still, we find calling ducks to be much more exciting and gratifying. It requires more skill, and it also extends the duration of the excitement by keeping us involved in the process. Calling also helps prove that hunting is not simply a matter of luck; the use of a call is testimony to the active, critical role the hunter plays.

A hunter can derive satisfaction and enjoyment from practicing with calls. I love to call both while hunting and in the evening at home. I am not a musician, but I believe the "running" of a call is analogous to playing an instrument. The very act of doing it is enjoyable, and probably therapeutic.

The importance of turkey calls can be illustrated by an experience I had with two turkey hunters for whom I have the greatest respect, Jerry Rodgers and Hearl Kelly. (These two wonderful characters are described in more depth in the chapter Only in America.) Hearl was entering a calling contest that demanded the use of a box call. I offered him a superb call that Dennis Poeschel had built for me in 1998. Hearl was very sensitive to the fact that there could be some risk to the call if he took it to the contest. Jerry, Hearl, and I all believed that this particular call was one of those one-in-a-thousand items that by chance was simply a bit better than the other great calls Dennis had made of the same materials and to the same dimensions. The importance of the call was put in perspective when Hearl said, "You know, John, there is no guarantee that the call will survive the trip! I might be in a terrible automobile accident on the way to the contest. Think what a loss it would be *if the call were crushed!*" Jerry added, "Can you imagine how Hearl would feel if he destroyed that call in an accident, John?"

All I can add to this is that the box did have incredible tone. And it did survive the trip. Hearl placed second in a contest among scores of great callers.

Another index to the importance of turkey calls is the amount of money a dedicated hunter invests in them. If you're a committed hunter, you know that that new call just might be better than the ones you have. You *have* to try it. I am sure there are some very grim stories of turkey hunters taking the money that was allocated for the baby's milk to buy yet another call. I have a pretty good story myself.

The main character is an intelligent man who, at the time of the incident, was in his twenties with a wife and young child. He was, and remains, an avid turkey hunter. Spring hunting was a passion. I have seen others whose lives were comparably impacted by the activity, but never one who became addicted quicker.

He wanted all the best gear. We were concerned about his compulsiveness because he had a modest income and all the financial challenges that the head of a young family faces. One of the first clues to his willingness to spend money was the purchase of a double-barreled Beretta 10-gauge shotgun. I had one, and he thought it was the perfect turkey gun. He found one of these rather rare guns and paid a premium price for it. His greatest weakness, though, was turkey calls. He bought every call he could find.

The story begins when I bought my first Neal Cost box call. It was 1980, and we were naively shocked by its high price tag: thirty-five dollars. How I wish I had had the foresight to purchase twenty of them! Before I showed the beautiful, and highly functional, call to Jim, I demonstrated it to a few good friends. They were all impressed by the tone.

I began to wonder: Could I *afford* to show it to Jim? If he heard it, no budget that he and Betty had established would keep him from buying one. A mutual friend named Jesse and I decided we should not tell Jim about the call. Unfortunately, a third friend told Jim he had heard us making some incredible calls one evening on "a box call." That same evening I was just sitting down to dinner when Jim bolted through the door, and said, with no salutations or greetings to Nell or the girls, "What about this box that Franke heard you and Suber using?" Nell teased him by saying, "Hello, Jim, are we interested in this call?" My two young daughters just looked up with disbelief at yet another of their father's strange friends. Jim's basic gentleness and good manners quickly returned, and he said, "Sorry, Nell. I heard this call was incredible." Nell just smiled and said, "Really." Fortunately I had to meet with some students, so I was able to tell Jim that I would have to show him the call the next day. Jim, embarrassed by his assault on our home, did not press. After dinner, I called Jesse and we discussed strategies for saving Jim from himself.

Jesse and I decided we had to trick our friend into thinking we did not have a new call but had learned of an incredible method for *tuning* an old box. It seemed like a long shot, but we decided to give the deception a try in the interest of Jim's financial well-being. We still faced the challenge of convincing Jim we had dramatically changed the box by simply "tuning" it.

"This is going to have to involve some fairly major deception, my man," Jesse said. "Jim is too knowledgeable to buy the idea that we just sanded the side of the box." I agreed and said we would have to come up with something really creative. Much to my wife's horror—I now publicly admit the idea was mine—I said to Jesse, "Suppose we told him you have to use human urine on the paddle of the box to break down the buildup of chalk? We could say that only urine has the chemical content to *totally* remove the residue of the old chalk."

Jesse stared. "No way would he buy that!"

I insisted that there was a chance. I knew Jim would do anything to obtain the perfect call. The diabolical plan was set in motion.

Our first step was to thoroughly remove the chalk, in a conventional manner, from an old box that Jim knew I had. I would use one of our many joint morning scouting expeditions to demonstrate the call to Jim under the proper conditions, which meant outside and at some distance. (We had learned that we could never achieve a true tone from a call indoors.) I would hide the new Cost box in my pack as I carried the "treated" old call in my hand. After getting out of Jim's sight, I would pull out the Cost box and use it. A key element in the strategy would be my need to rush off to class immediately, leaving Jim no time to make a couple of quick strokes on the "treated" box. We also decided to tell Jim he had to heat the box in a 150-degree oven for three minutes after applying the urine.

When I told Nell about our plan, she said, "No, John, you can't do that!" I argued that it was for the economic welfare of Jim's family. She did not press the discussion.

You can guess the rest. Jim fell for it *hook, line, and sinker.* We even had the good fortune of enlisting a mutual friend to follow Jim home for the treatment of the call. Parker watched Jim enter the bathroom, then come out gingerly holding a very wet call. Only when Jim opened the oven to insert the call did Parker tap him on the shoulder and say, "Sorry, Mr. Adams, I am afraid that the good doctor and Suber got you."

Jim was not a happy turkey hunter when he realized what his "friends" had done. I was so embarrassed that for years I never shared the story with anyone outside our small group of sensitive friends. At this point, however—almost twenty years after the ultimate turkey-hunting practical joke was perpetrated—I think the world needs to know what an obsessive turkey hunter will do to get a better call.

36

DIVERSE BACKGROUNDS— COMMON OBSESSIONS

When you see a turkey hunter carrying a bird from the woods, it will not be easy to define who he is. Turkey hunters come from diverse backgrounds—racially, ethnically, socioeconomically, physically, philosophically, and occupationally. Such diversity is not seen in all groups pursuing outdoor activities; on the contrary, many seem to attract the same types of people. Look at those who pursue grouse and trout. I have scores of friends who are both avid grouse hunters and trout anglers. There seem to be common themes in the way in which they are selected by the activity: Most, for instance, are well educated and like to read.

Or look at great bass fishermen. The guys who become the most successful competitive bass anglers seem to come from similar cultural backgrounds.

Turkey hunters are different. When I think about the best turkey hunters I have known, the diversity is incredible: stockbroker, Nease; anesthesiologist, Triplett; factory shift worker, Rodgers; coach, Franke; well digger, Leizer; forest service biologist, Saunders; teacher, Tiberio; attorney, Suber; fuel oil distributor, Fleenor; sign maker, Johenning; stonemason-musician, Pruett; archaeologist, Adams; New York financier, Monier; mechanic, Podlejski; sawmill laborer, Kelly; forester, Thayer; urologist, Buckley; musician, Leva.

It is also revealing to look at the names in the above list. They reveal cultural ties to many parts of the world—another chapter in the story of the red, white, and blue melting pot. From this small occupational sample alone you'll find ancestors from Norway, Sweden, France, England, Ireland, Scotland, Italy, Germany, Poland . . . and this is just my sample. Every avid hunter will have his own list of names.

Remember those World War II movies that depicted American units? The scriptwriter always chose ethnically diverse names for the characters in the platoon. But this diversity was not created by screenwriters; it was there when the ammunition was live. Look at the names on the endless crosses in the cemetery above Normandy's beaches. The men who waded onto French soil and pushed the Germans back across the Rhine, had ancestors from all over the world. In many cases the last names were the same as those of the enemy. Others were as French as the people they came to liberate.

Moreover, my sample is from one *small* area in western Virginia. Many of these hunters, or their parents, immigrated to our mountains from other parts of America. In fact most of them did not have grandparents native to the areas they now hunt. My partner came from Minnesota, but don't let anyone tell me that his ancestors' long stay in the heartland made it impossible for him to be as skillful a hunter as anyone here.

The diversity reflects the mobility that defines American subcultures. For a number of years turkey hunting was the domain of southern hunters. That has changed. Today, where a man comes from cannot be used as a clue to his avocations. Now the great hunters and callers come from all across our huge nation. Some western states have only recently provided turkey-hunting opportunities. I remember when the great Idaho angler Mike Lawson told me he was going on his first turkey hunt. I had a hunch he would be hooked. Now I feel sorry for the western turkeys that have to face him, and his brother and sons.

I love the variations in socioeconomic backgrounds that exist among *great* turkey hunters. The groups selects its best performers from both the rich and the poor. I remember a turkey-hunting friend being incredulous at what he saw as the exorbitant price of sixty-five dollars charged for a motel room when he went to a calling contest. At the same competition another friend, and an equally obsessive turkey hunter, told me about a twenty-acre lot for sale near his home in Jackson, Wyoming. The price tag was $3,000,000.00. If you have trouble counting the zeros, that is three million dollars for twenty acres of what was marginal cattle range twenty years ago. Both these guys are *great* turkey hunters. If they hunted together, they would get along well, yet the differences between their respective financial statuses could not be greater. Wealth does not determine membership in this select company. Nor can you predict how individuals will hunt based on their means. Toughness is not the exclusive domain of any socioeconomic group.

In many cases the nonhunting interests of the great hunters are very diverse. A few of the best are addicted to NASCAR racing. Others cannot understand the appeal of car races. Some are fanatical fans of team sports, others have absolutely no interest. Musical taste, or total lack thereof, is another disparity. I have seen many who were as devoted to the traditional music of the mountains in which we hunt as they are to the wild turkeys. Others can't stand it. A few have a commitment to classical music. One great hunter loves the theater; others would not even *consider* going. Some like to dance, others never have. A few are avid readers, others read nothing but the sports pages. Most would not be caught in a museum, several seek them out. A vacation for some means Disney World; for others, a remote lake; and for a few, a major city.

Racial diversity is part of the great story. I remember when I was trying to peddle my first turkey-hunting book at civic meetings in western Virginia. In most cases the audiences were exclusively white. Once when I was signing books, I looked up to see a proud-looking black man in front of me. He was quiet, but his eyes burned with freedom. It took courage to enter the shabby gym that for years had been FOR WHITES ONLY. In the hardwoods no one wrote those three words on the trees. When he picked up his book, he looked me in the eye and said, "Your tube calling is the best I have ever heard." I am as proud of the compliment now as I was fifteen years ago when the soft-spoken man made it. I hope to encounter him in the woods someday.

There are immense educational differences among the characters who hunt wild turkeys, too. I have hunted with men who hold the most prestigious degrees that our nation can award. I have hunted with others who never finished high school. One couldn't sign his name. Communication between those of such different educational backgrounds is not impossible. When it comes to hunting the wild turkey, we all speak the same language.

The obsession provides its own subcultural language. Yes, it is a type of English, but it is the lexicon of the turkey hunter. It has created words such as *gang, scatter, jake, jenny, run* (used as a verb and meaning "to use a call"), *hammer* (again, used as a verb), *slate, glass, striker, bone, sign* . . . As is the case with many other subcultural lingos, it has produced its own grammatical rules. For example, how many "normal" Americans would understand the following sentence: "He has been hammered all season. I would only tree-call at flying-down time. If he didn't come back, I would just cluck and purr."

There is certainly no religious group common to wild-turkey hunters. I have pursued the birds with as broad a cross section of religious affiliations as you can imagine. Some, including ministers, are as committed to formal religion as anyone can be; others have no affiliation at all.

There is great age variation among turkey hunters. I love the tough old guys who still climb the ridges. I have encountered many in their seventies who still go after them with determination and skill. There is so much to learn you cannot expect to have the answers until you gain some maturity. In fact, some of the best hunters I know are retired. They may not cover as much ground as the tough college kid, but they make a hell of a lot fewer mistakes.

A lot of avid turkey hunters are very different in appearance, and the physical variations are not simply a function of ethnic or racial diversity. Unlike the case of some team sports, large size is not an advantage in turkey hunting. Strength is helpful, and some great hunters are big men; however, small stature and a lack of mass makes it easier to face the physical strain of walking long distances over tough terrain. It is a simple equation: No matter how strong you are, it is more difficult to pull 250 pounds up the steep slopes than it is to pull 150 pounds. It does not take a huge body to carry an eight-pound gun, hence a lot of the hunters who cover the most ground are small. Still, they come in all physical types. One of the best hunters I know is six foot seven; another equally skilled hunter is five foot three. If you saw them together, you might wonder if they were on break from a carnival. It is also not a sport that selects only for those who live in fitness gyms. Yes, some of the best are lean and in good physical condition, but others enjoy eating and do not look like well-trained athletes. I know one who has so many muscles that he looks as if he could compete in the bodybuilding contests. His hunting partner looks as if he spends most of his time on a couch and would not be *allowed* in the fitness gym. The odd couple make a great team in the field.

Political and philosophical differences are profound. Many pieces in this book indicate my respect and admiration for my hunting partner, Gary. Politically, we are far apart. My political hero is Robert Kennedy; his is Ronald Reagan. His philosophical orientation is tied to the conservative values of the midwestern heartland in which he grew up and where his family farmed. My liberal orientation was seeded by an Ivy League community in the Northeast, where my father was a professor and he and my mother championed all the liberal causes. Our love for hunting the wild turkey created bonds that are as close as can exist between two men.

The variations in personal style and dress are also remarkable. Turkey hunters can dress in all Brooks Brothers or all

Farmer's Co-op. Some guys never wear a tie, others are rarely without one. I have friends who are never without boots, while others wear them only when they hunt. Some are covered with facial hair, others as clean-cut as a Marine Corps company of Korean War vintage.

The case for the great diversity among turkey hunters must be viewed with care. There are Americans or, more accurately, groups of Americans who are but rarely represented. My list of the best hunters in my small area of Virginia, for instance, has no females. They *will* be on it in the future, and some of the female pioneers out there are as good as any of the men on my list; however, at this juncture in western Virginia, they are not part of the population. The reason is straightforward: American cultures have discouraged women from becoming hunters. The process begins when parents select toys for their children on the basis of their sex: They buy Barbie dolls for Mary, GI Joe soldiers for James.

An insight came to me as I reflected on the question of diversity: My list of great hunters includes no Jewish names. At first I thought I must have overlooked someone. After all, the great Jewish character is always an integral part of the platoon in the World War II flicks. Also, all the athletic teams I participated on had important Jewish members. Also, I have many Jewish friends who fly fish in the West with me. As hard as I searched, though, no Jewish turkey hunters emerged. I wonder if the essentially urban experience of Jewish Americans makes them less likely to be attracted to hunting?

In conclusion, it seems fitting that the most distinctively American form of hunting demonstrates the same diversity that is at the heart of our nation. It may be unfair, but I also believe that the diversity has contributed to the remarkable range of problem-solving talents brought to the special challenges of wild-turkey hunting.

37

ONLY IN AMERICA

This piece is a tribute to two superb turkey hunters who live in the James River Valley of Virginia. Jerry Rodgers and Hearl Kelly are an important part of the American story. I would never have met either man if I had not written a book on turkey hunting. One March evening in 1982 I was practicing calls when the phone rang. I picked it up to hear Hearl say, "Mr. McDaniel, Jerry and I liked your book and would like to talk to you." I invited them to come to our home the next evening.

When they arrived, it was clear they had come for one reason: to talk about wild turkeys. As would be the case in all our future visits, we went to my gun room and talked about nothing but turkey hunting and running calls. My friends have always been very polite to my wife and daughters; it is just that the purpose of their visits is clear. We usually spend from two to five hours in the room.

I share little in common with Hearl and Jerry. Both men are younger than I am and work as laborers: Hearl in a lumber mill, Jerry in a school bus factory. Neither man had the opportunity for advanced education, and neither has traveled extensively. A shared passion for hunting the wild turkey brought us together. The bond I feel with them is deeper than what I feel with my academic colleagues who have histories and professional interests similar to my own. The respect and admiration I have for the two men could not be deeper.

The stories they tell are always true, even when they are hard on their reputations. Jerry was once involved in a nonfatal hunting accident, and he talks about it with candor. This honesty extends to failures. In fact, many of their best stories are about their setbacks in the turkey woods. At times each of us simply has a terrible year. One year Jerry went from one frustration to another while Hearl and I were having success. Jerry never got upset or jealous. I hope that I matched the manner in which Hearl responded to Jerry's hard luck: There was no false sympathy, no hidden enjoyment of his setbacks, no underlying smirk that said, "Well, you had some good years but now this will even it up." I have seen that from some friends when I have had bad years. They can't hide their enjoyment at my suffering a bit. That is not true of Jerry and Hearl.

Hearl has hunted all his life, but when we met it was clear that he had not had much experience wingshooting. When he talked about his experience with a poorly balanced single-shot 10-gauge shotgun he had purchased for turkey hunting, he was brutally honest about his lack of success.

Jerry and Hearl pull no punches about those who don't measure up. The name of a local guy who took people turkey hunting for a fee once came up. They both said with cold honesty, "He can't call." It was not mean, it was just a simple fact stated by guys who *knew*.

The passion they have for hunting the wild turkey is limitless. They hunt when they are ill, injured, or in tough financial straits. Only a family tragedy or terrible health problem will keep them from the field.

I can still see Hearl's face, flushed with excitement, as he said, "I've got *five* weeks to go after them starting Saturday. I'm ready to rock and roll!" As he said it, he virtually screamed with the joy of having the time to do that what he enjoys doing more than anything in the world.

I remember Jerry's passion when I expressed my condolences upon hearing that he had been laid off from his job. His response was, "Yeah, I have to find another job, but right now it gives me more time to go after them!"

Few nonhunters would believe the range of knowledge and skill Jerry and Hearl have acquired as a function of their hobbies. Their understanding of the flora and fauna of the woods is vast; I would like to see a biologist compete with them concerning their respective knowledge of plants eaten by wild turkeys. And throw out the name of *any* modern rifle—Jerry will tell you the handload it shoots best. He will tell you how many grains of powder, what make of bullet, and which primer you should use in the load. He will not make the statement with arrogance, but with the quiet confidence of having tested it. I would put Jerry's knowledge of guns designed for hunting up against anyone's.

Jerry has searched hard to find the perfect shotgun for buckshot. He has tried every gun, barrel length, and choke in his endless search to find *the* gun. One episode is instructive. Jerry's hunt camp borders one that is used exclusively by blacks. Jerry says there was no interaction between the two groups until the day he met one of the black hunters while walking the property line. Jerry instantly noticed the hunter had an old Browning Auto-5 with the same thirty-two-inch barrel that Jerry uses. The two hunters began to talk about the great Auto–5s they both loved. They talked for a long time and agreed to extend the discussion. Mutual respect for the great shotgun created a bond that resulted in both groups overcoming prejudices that were decades old.

Hearl does not have the ballistic knowledge of Jerry, but his calling skills put him into a very select group. He frequently wins contests even though he competes against men whose sole occupation is making and using calls. Hearl's desire to become a great caller is almost obsessive. He carries a call in his mouth all the time. I suspect he drives his coworkers crazy. I am sure his wife has heard more turkey calls than any woman in the world. He even raises young turkeys so he can have the sound around him all the time. Why the calls became such an important part of his life remains a wonderful mystery. I cannot imagine how many hours Hearl has spent with his calls; I know my more modest skills involved an investment of time that still had the members of my family shaking their heads in disbelief. On one occasion a very bright student of mine came to our home on one of the nights that Jerry, Hearl, and I were together. The student is not a turkey hunter, but after spending an evening with us, he said, "Hearl is a virtuoso." He is.

And remember, all the knowledge and skill demonstrated by these men is generated by a *hobby*. It could have been time spent on the golf course. Instead these guys went out and became anonymous experts on the wild turkey. They have received dividends beyond the obvious enjoyment of the sport. They are known as great turkey hunters. More important, they know that they are part of a small group that meets the challenge of this game consistently. Their jobs provide little satisfaction or public respect. I believe that turkey hunting has added something very important to their sense of self-esteem. Many people in the area call Hearl "Turkey." It is a nickname we all enjoy. Those who care—and there are many in the ridges and valleys of western Virginia who do—know Hearl and Jerry are the very best.

These guys are kind and generous as well. One summer Jerry became very ill and was hospitalized. Hearl was there to help him in any way he could. He took care of Jerry's yard and visited him regularly in the hospital. When Hearl's home burned down, Jerry was there to offer support.

On one occasion I was having trouble finding some bullets for a .22 Hornet I was handloading. Jerry had told me about some old Winchester 45-grain soft points that were no longer available, so I asked him if he could suggest anything that shot about as well. He said he had never found a bullet that was as accurate or as effective on wild turkeys as the Winchesters. The next time he came to visit, he had a large bag of his precious life-time supply of the discontinued bullets for me. He insisted I take them, despite my protests.

On another occasion I had been using a Benelli automatic for a couple of years. Jerry asked me about the gun and said he was considering buying one. I told him to use mine to see if liked it. This good friend simply said, "I don't think it is appropriate to borrow a man's guns, John." The attitude did not surprise me. I have lent guns to a lot of friends, and I respect Jerry's position.

You earn the reputation of being a great turkey hunter. Some of the great ones have had easy lives; the majority, how-ever, are like Hearl and Jerry—guys who derive modest incomes from tedious jobs. Many were even deprived of the fleeting, glo-rious moments in their youth when they could run through the other towns' boys carrying a football. Jerry and Hearl were working, or hunting, to help feed their families when the other boys were practicing useless skills.

I remember one night when my big Chesapeake, Sage, was in the house when Jerry and Hearl arrived. The dog sensed these were good guys and spent the entire evening getting close to them. She would put her head on their laps and reach up to touch them with her paw. They both responded with warmth and respect. They not only tolerated the dog, but enjoyed her. The day before I had a very successful attorney in my home; I had to put Sage outside because he had no time for her, and she was not ready to tolerate him. Chesapeakes are probably better judges of character than most humans.

Our special nation allowed these men to develop their hunting skills. When they got really good at it, some honest guys came to them for counsel. Jerry and Hearl were no longer "the guys who work at the mill" but, rather, "the great turkey hunters." Not the good old fat boys who scored touchdowns back in 1955, but the men who always kill them *now*.

You can't fake turkey hunting. You have to be good at it, be-cause this is not a popularity contest. If you start calling yourself a turkey hunter, you have to produce or the quiet, bright guys will know. The boss may not like you, but that makes no difference.

I told Hearl and Jerry about a friend who had risen rapidly in the academic community. One interesting habit he had was leaving the light on in his office in the evening. My partner and I were sure it was done to convince people he was in his office for extended periods of time. Jerry said simply, "That boy may get to be dean, but he will never kill gobblers consistently."

Some may try. They will stop you and ask if you will listen to their calls. They will make a few notes and you will know. It is not they have not a made an effort; they just don't understand the *commitment* it takes. Some will buy all the right stuff, learn the language, and work at it a bit. The problem is that the wild turkey is more difficult to fool than the president, dean, deacon, or boss. There are arenas where you can be glib, look good, get in late and leave early, and prosper. Just take a deep breath and think about it before you try to use the same strategies and work ethic to compete with Jerry and Hearl in the field.

They do not tolerate fools or the morally corrupt. On one occasion they came to my home just after President Clinton had been impeached. Before their arrival, Nell and I had watched the evening news and been appalled by polls suggesting most Americans did not care about Clinton's admitted transgressions and deceitfulness. We were more horrified by the evidence that feminist groups seemed to be making excuses for his actions. Hearl, Jerry, and I rarely talk politics, but on this evening I enjoyed the fact they made it clear that the polls were not correct when it came to the two of them.

Jerry and Hearl are real. They would have been there with their quiet courage when the crop didn't come up, or when the kids didn't get well, or when ordered to run into the merciless fire on Omaha Beach. They don't see themselves as American heroes, but it is Jerry and Hearl who keep the fire alive in the land of the free and home of the brave.

38

THE DUEL

The appeals of turkey hunting are many. One of the most captivating is the one-on-one duel. The best duels are the most
difficult. We all enjoy the occasional quick success; however, the
greatest satisfaction is provided by the excruciatingly difficult
situation.

I had a great one yesterday. I hunted a small farm we own
on Buffalo Creek in Rockbridge County, Virginia. The general
area has received intense hunting pressure over the last five
years. I went because a friend had told me that there was an "impossible" gobbler on the border between his property and ours.

The first gobble was at 6:07 A.M. I got in position and made
a few soft clucks on one of my favorite calls, a glass friction call
made by D. D. Adams in 1987. At 6:18, a few minutes after my
initial calls, he gobbled from the ground, at a distance of about
125 yards. He was located in a small bowl below the prominent
ridge on which I had set up. After five minutes I made a few soft

yelps. The bird did not respond. Several minutes later he began to gobble and continued to do so from the same general location until 7. During this same period I made a number of calls. He did not respond to any of them. At 7 I decided to go silent to see if he might become impatient. From 7 until 7:20 I did not make a call, and he began to gobble more aggressively. (If your experience with calling to mature gobblers is limited, let me respectfully suggest that a twenty-minute wait to call can seem like a *very* long time.) I was confident he was on his way when he suddenly quit gobbling at 7:25. I had my gun up and was waiting to hear his footsteps. Nothing. At 7:40 I couldn't stand it and made a quick yelp—no response. I began to try other calls. Each was met with silence. Now, suspecting he was gone, I decided to move to a knoll on the other side of the bowl. I did not walk through the bowl, but rather around it on a small half-moon-shaped ridge that joined the two knolls. I called from the new position at 7:55. Nothing. I used different calls—now a wingbone and a tube. I had no answer for a full half hour. At 8:25 I was sure I was finished, but not having heard another bird, I decided to return to my original location to call again.

Despite my lack of confidence, I moved as silently as possible, keeping the contour of the small ridge between me and the position from which the turkey had last gobbled in the bowl. I arrived at my original location at 8:45 and immediately began some aggressive hen calling. Nothing. In desperation, I considered imitating a gobbler fight. I smiled to myself as I prepared to make the unorthodox call because I knew my good friend, and great turkey hunter, Hearl Kelly would not approve. He had spent more than a month testing gobbler-fighting calls and was convinced that their effectiveness had been dramatically exaggerated. I had not bought one of the new calls, but for years had used a D. D. Adams slate call to make the aggressive purring sounds. I told Hearl that I figured I had success with the call about 10 percent of the time I used it. Hearl said, "Hell, John, I do a lot better than that with any call!" I used the call when things got very tough. This was one of those times.

I combined the aggravated purr with an imitation of the gobble on my Morgan tube call. As soon as I began the aggressive purring I was greeted with a robust gobble from the exact place where the bird had been an hour and a half before. The gobbler began to gobble incessantly as I made the harsh purring sounds. I called until my hand cramped on the striker. Despite his constant gobbling, the turkey would not move.

It was now 9:15. I decided to try moving on the bird. My plan was to call while moving back down the half-moon ridge. As I began to move and call, the gobbling became even more aggressive. By 9:35, though, the turkey had cut back on the frequency and intensity of his calling.

At this juncture I reflected on what a wonderful morning it had been. The duel with the bird, which I was sure I was about to lose, had been captivating. Still, I decided to try one final tactic. I would move, make a single cluck, and then wait until the bird came or until the legal shooting time expired at noon. As I crawled to my final position, the bird gobbled again. I set up against a small tree and made a single soft cluck. Nothing. It was 9:45. The bird did not make another gobble, but I sensed he was coming. Several minutes later I heard the sound of footsteps. They were not the steady cadence of a bird coming confidently, but rather the slow, deliberate pace of a stalking predator. I wondered if it might be a bobcat. The first thing I saw was the bright *red* head of a gobbler low to the ground and sneaking, a step at a time, toward me. I remember thinking he looked like a snake as he slithered toward me low to the ground. At twenty-five yards he went behind a small tree, and I shifted my gun slightly. When he snuck out from behind the tree, I felt calm as I pressed the trigger. The great bird flopped on the ground and I stood, knowing he was head-shot. I looked at my watch: 9:50. The duel had lasted three hours and thirty-two minutes. The bird—which I expected to be huge—was, for our area, of average size at seventeen pounds, twelve ounces. He had an ordinary ten-inch beard and one-inch spurs. He may not have been the largest of gobblers, but he was special.

I was confident that this bird was the "impossible gobbler" my friend had identified. What made him so difficult? I do not have an answer. I looked for old shot wounds but found none. (I have found shot, or the evidence of shotgun wounds, on four birds I have killed.) I suspect that the bird had been hunted intensely, called to frequently, and probably shot at.

The three-and-a-half-hour duel had involved a number of strategies. I had called from eight different locations. The inventory of calls I used included a Dick Kirby box, a Raymond Chisholm aluminum call, a D. D. Adams glass, a Ken Morgan tube, a Rich Tiberio wingbone, a Tom Fleenor wingbone, and a diaphragm. I had used some of the calls for more than twenty years.

As I carried the bird off the small hill, I thought of how lucky we are to have the opportunity to hunt these great creatures. You can pay thousands of dollars and travel thousands of miles to hunt the most prestigious game of the world, but none will provide a better duel than the one I just described. I eliminate no game creature from consideration. Go ahead and throw in your "dangerous" game. If you take a longbow, I will listen to your story with admiration. But most will not take longbows; they carry modern rifles with four thousand foot-pounds of energy and a scope that lets you count the whiskers on an animal. They are "carried" by White Hunters who offer protection in the remote chance of trouble. The poor buffalo or lion really doesn't have a chance. It will be no duel.

Stay at home, save the ten thousand dollars, and see if you, alone, are capable of dealing with a particularly tough wild turkey gobbler.

39

PULLING THE BAITS

At one stage in a life committed to the outdoors, I became addicted to fishing from a small boat off Cape Hatteras. It was a classic seventeen-foot, six-inch Boston Whaler. I shared her with the woman I wanted to spend my life with.

Early in our career with the Whaler, I sought advice from the experienced captains who fished out of Hatteras Village. One was reputed to be the best. Nell said he looked like a raccoon because of the way the sun had burned his face: The only part that was not dark tan was a masklike area protected by his sunglasses. I remember seeing the guy at the Atlantic View Restaurant early each morning, waiting for his clients. He never looked happy. I always listened, with a childish intensity, to what he had to say. Once a loud client said to him, "I can't wait to go! I love to catch marlin more than anything in the world!" The captain's comment has implications for turkey hunters. He said, in a perfect Outer Banks accent: "You had better enjoy pulling the baits, because there will be a lot of time between marlin."

If you are ready to commit yourself to wild-turkey hunting, you had better enjoy "pulling the baits," too, because there will be a lot of time between turkeys. It is important to recognize what the dour captain was trying to communicate to the loud client. Defining *success* as "the catching of the fish" or "the killing of the turkey" is a mistake. To love the sport, you have to enjoy the labor. It is the process itself that becomes captivating.

I love to call turkeys. I think that statement is often misinterpreted to suggest I enjoy killing the turkeys that come to my calls. That is incorrect. I love the *process* of calling. I take pride in making good calls. I am not interested in entering contests to prove my calling skill, I just love to call. Do not misunderstand me: I am not suggesting that my skills are comparable to those of the great contest callers. They clearly are not. I am simply very comfortable with my level of competence.

I also enjoy the arduous search, even when I am not rewarded with finding birds. A hard day is a joy. I can feel very satisfied if I have held to a tough plan and invested a good hunt. To enjoy it, you have to be doing it well, with the correct "baits" deployed and all your gear working as it should. If you get lazy and do a poor job of pulling the baits, the day will be terrible.

It is not simply a function of the effort you make. You need a correct mind-set. If you are desperate to kill a turkey, you are jeoparidzing the joys of the hunt. You will not enjoy the woods as you do when you are relaxed. That does not suggest that you have to develop an "I don't care if I kill one" attitude. Let me remind you: The man at Hatteras was the most productive captain in the area. There can be a balance. The turkey, or the marlin, has to be important.

One of the most enjoyable aspects of pulling the baits for me has been observing turkeys. I love to watch the beautiful hens. I marvel at their ability to raise young turkeys. Hen turkeys are legal in our fall season, but I rarely kill them. I love to watch them and take pride in the fact that a personal commitment to killing gobblers only must be helping the population.

I enjoy seeing not only hen turkeys but also all the other creatures, large and small, that share the ridges and hollows with them. On six occasions I have had the thrilling experience of seeing black bears at close range. I have enjoyed watching the antics of baby squirrels in the spring, and marveled at the speed of accipiter hawks as they darted through the fall hardwoods. I love the flora of the area as well. I know where there are huge oaks that have fortuitously escaped being cut because they were on property lines. I look forward to seeing them each time I hunt the properties that maintain them.

I love the colors of the fall hardwood forests: the reds, coppers, tans, golds, browns, yellows, rusts, maroons, and shades in between. The subtle variations in the conifers' greens add a striking contrast to the brilliant leaves of the deciduous trees.

I doubt if a tape of fall hardwood sounds is being marketed, but I'd buy one if it were. I am not talking about the many thrilling calls wild turkeys make, but rather the other sounds of the woods: the chatter of squirrels, the distant calls of geese, the guttural tones of ravens, and the raucous calls of crows. I never appreciated how important the common calls of crows were until my daughter phoned from New York City after two months on her first job. A crow outside our Virginia house was audible to her on the telephone, and she said, "Oh, I miss the sound of the crows." When you are pulling the baits you have the opportunity to see, hear, and smell so much.

Intense commitment to an activity gives you immense freedom. When you are involved in the pursuit, not many things intrude. The captain is in charge of his boat. The turkey hunter sets the agenda for a day in the field. The freedom is real. I love to plan hunts. An important part of effective hunting or fishing is making adjustments in your plans. I certainly cannot relate to the many types of data the captain must use as he alters his plans during a long day at sea, but I am sure there are similarities in the process.

I enjoy a full day of walking. Turkey hunting will tax your stamina. When you feel yourself meeting the challenges of the hunt, it provides satisfaction. You can feel your own strength, but you can also recognize when you have developed such skills as keeping your balance on tough slopes.

I suspect the arduous parts of the process works to relax your mind and body. Most of us are probably in need of more physical activity for the welfare of our minds. I know I am most relaxed after a hard day in the field.

Finding your way is part of pulling the baits. I remember a day when heavy fog moved in on the mountain and visibility was limited to less than fifty feet. I somehow found my way to the spot from which I wanted to listen; the modest navigational accomplishment gave me great pride. I never heard a turkey that day but the pulling of the baits was particularly gratifying.

Becoming efficient with the tools is part of pulling the baits. I am not interested in competing in the shooting sports, but I would be embarrassed to see a record of the hours I have allocated to working with my shotguns. The work has involved not just practice with the guns, but also the time-consuming development of loads and never-ending quest for a more efficient gun, barrel, or choke tube. Part of it is the need to kill as cleanly as possible. Another component is the simple joy in being good at something. I remember the surprise and pride I felt when my partner was talking to me about a crazy friend he had as a kid. The point of the story was the unusual, in fact outrageous, behavior of the bizarre kid, but as an aside Gary said, "Yeah, he was crazy, but until I met you, he was the best wingshot I had ever seen." I work hard at my wingshooting. There is no monetary reward, and most people I meet will neither know nor care about the level of skill I have developed. To me, it is an important part of pulling the baits.

Adjusting to the weather is part of pulling the baits. I enjoy feeling the efficiency of the clothes and boots that human intelligence has created. Certain garments become important parts of your inventory of critical items. The effective choice and use of great equipment has an appeal of its own.

Late one day when my partner and I had just begun to hunt together, Gary came to the tree stand in which I had been sitting watching a deer scrape for two days. It was late November and it had snowed all day. I had not moved from the stand since climbing into it at 5:30 A.M. When Gary saw me, my hat had several inches of snow on it, and I remember him saying, "If this is what it takes to kill a trophy buck, I am not sure I am ready to make the commitment!" My wonderful equipment had made it possible to endure the cold; however, I was proud of what it had demanded of me. Endurance and determination are part of pulling the baits.

Those of us who are addicted to a sport find the *entire experience* captivating. One question that may be logically raised, then, is that if killing is not what attracts and holds the hunter or angler, then why not just go out and enjoy great creatures by observing them? The answer lies in the intensity that the goal provides. You do not have to kill the turkey or subdue the marlin to enjoy the event, but you must seek the difficult goal. I have often said that it is more difficult to take good photographs of wild turkeys than it is to kill them. That is true, but the process of photographing them does not provide the heart-pounding excitement that is there when you are trying to kill one.

If the camera is moved when you hit the shutter, you will produce a poor photograph, but you will not be traumatized by the knowledge that the beautiful creature could be crippled by poorly placed shot. Performing with poise and skill is demanded by the responsibility you have to the animal you love. The human nervous system does not take killing large animals or birds easily. You will be tight with anticipation, and coping with that anxiety is part of the process. In the case of the marlin release— and unlike the turkey photograph—you have in fact brought the fish to the boat. You have accomplished everything that you would have done if you had decided to keep him.

From a different perspective, many dedicated turkey hunters do not understand why some hunters seem to enjoy shortcutting the process of pulling the baits. Driving a pickup truck through fields "hunting" for deer may be legal, but it detracts from those elements of the hunting that are most enjoyable. The truck insulates you from the natural world that is at the core of why so many of us love to hunt. In addition, there is none of hunting's satisfaction from meeting the challenges of hard physical work. You may argue that road hunting is popular among those whose jobs do not leave them enough time to invest in other types of hunting. I am not ready to concede that point. I have friends who have the time to hunt in a more involved manner, but instead will simply drive through fields. My argument has nothing to do with the productivity of the technique. Driving through fields can be very productive—you cover a lot of ground, and deer that live on farms are accustomed to seeing pickup trucks. The critical point is that the simplistic method undermines the process.

It is difficult for people who do not hunt to understand that for the true hunter it is the *process* that is at the core of the activity. Pulling the baits is the process. The goal, killing or bringing the game to hand, imposes critical thrills, but it is the journey we relish.

40

SACRED PLACES IN THE PROMISED LAND

Our country is immense and affords great diversity in habitats. We have seen declines in our game populations as a function of habitat destruction, but we have not seen the devastation that has taken place in many countries of Europe, Asia, and South America. For the avid hunter, the United States remains a promised land.

Let us not forget that turkeys evolved only in the Americas. They exist nowhere else. From the perspective of the wild turkey, this is indeed the promised land. Turkeys exploit so many different environments in America. You can hunt them in hardwoods, high plains, tropical swamps, and deserts. Yes, *deserts*. I will never forget the shock I felt when I flew into San Angelo, Texas, for what would be a wonderful spring hunt. From the plane, I could not believe turkeys could survive in the bleak-looking terrain. I have never seen as many turkeys as I did in that country.

Unlike many areas of the world, such as East Africa, we enjoy populations of game and birds that are higher than they were in the past. Citizens of the nineteenth-century East Coast would probably be amazed by current numbers of Canada geese, whitetails, and, wild turkeys in areas where they were rarely encountered before World War I.

If you live in or near an urban area, it may be hard to appreciate the natural vastness that remains in America. I'm speaking not just of Yellowstone and the other great parks but also of the huge tracts of public land that dominate the states of Wyoming, Idaho, and Montana. These areas are huge, and they protect game species. They are remote, and access is often not easy, but for the adventurous they offer another promised land.

Part of the great story is cultural: The promised land is not just the domain of the rich and famous. The vastness of the country was complemented by a democratic philosophy that said: We will protect this land for all Americans. We provided public parks and forests for all our citizens. It is not a Christian ethic or a Jewish ethic, nor is it a British or French ethic. It is an American ethic. And we should all remember the great Americans who had the courage and generosity of spirit to implement the protection. The selfishness that characterized the wealthy in so many nations from which our ancestors came was not maintained in America. Thanks to the democratic perspectives of great Americans, the great fishing and hunting areas were not destined to be private. The vast tracts of public property gave opportunities to anyone who had initiative.

Individual properties are part of the story of the promised land. You develop an attachment to the wonderful places. My hunting partner and I always harass each other for not finding new properties to hunt. But it is so hard not to go back to the places we know. You develop a commitment to the place, an intimacy with it, that drives you to go back to it time after time. It is as if it becomes a part of you. First the spot offers things that you enjoy—but then it captures you. Yes, you'll still look at other places, but it will be hard to leave yours.

I'm not just speaking of the places inhabited by wild turkeys. There is not a great turkey hunter who does not respect the other game in this nation. I can look at the pictures of hunters sitting in front of a huge elk, and marvel at the endless mountains in the background. I have the same attitude toward the small but precious woodlot in which the skilled squirrel hunter stalks his game. I love to see the pictures of the old waterfowl hunters who worked the Upper Chesapeake Bay. For them the promised land was the Susquehanna Flats, and what a place it must have been.

Every time I park my car in Last Chance, Idaho, and head down to the bank of the Henry's Fork, I shiver with excitement—*every* time. Idaho, Montana, Wyoming, Oregon, and Washington are blessed with great rivers. And for those of us fortunate enough to spend time there, it is a promised land.

In states such as New Jersey, there are tough guys who hunt with intensity and competence in the shadows of cities. I still remember the wonderful salt marsh around Atlantic City and the great brant I saw flying over the casinos there. The marsh, the brant, and the black ducks made that place a promised land. It was not Alaska or East Africa, but do not tell me that the boys over there are any better at their game or love their place any more than my friend Lou McFadden loves that marsh.

Show me a great turkey hunter and I will show you a person who loves his or her special sections of the promised land. To the hunter, such places become *sacred*. And I use that word with care. Many of those who bestow the word on places we love are not "religious" people. That is to say, we are not committed to conventional forms of religion. There are several reasons. First, none of the conventional religions has put a high enough priority on protecting the environment; second, most do not attribute importance to creatures other than man; finally, all exercise the arrogance that their particular culture and system of morality are inherently superior to all others.

You must be exposed to many forms of religious belief, particularly those of the American Indian, to begin to appreciate the respect other cultures have for the land. To many hunting cultures, natural areas were sacred. To the Sioux, for instance, no land could ever be the equivalent of the Black Hills.

It is this sacred spirit of places that is at the core of the respect hunters bring to a chosen area. The respect develops out of the intimacy for nature that is a necessary component of effective hunting. You must know a place well if you are to be effective there. While the achievement of intimacy is established for pragmatic reasons, it results in creating bonds with the land that become special.

Most American cultures value mobility and newness, and to many of us attachment to the land is beyond our ability to understand. If the price is right, we are ready to move on to another place. We focus on the monetary value of a piece of land rather than its sacred nature. That is essentially why the fight to protect the environment in the United States remains so difficult.

Show me men and women who love to hunt and fish and I will show you those who will be at the forefront of the effort to protect the natural environment. The intimacy that hunters and anglers feel with a place also makes them demand its protection. We still have sacred places to protect that are not part of large tracts of wilderness. They may be small—a tiny marsh or section of prairie that has escaped being cultivated—but they can be critical. The success of a true environmental ethic may depend on convincing a significant number of Americans that natural places are *sacred*.

41

THE LAST DAY

It had been a difficult year. My third spinal surgery resulted in my carrying pain into the field every day. The situation was compounded by our inability to find birds. Early in the fall we had seen large flocks, but as soon as the season opened they disappeared. During our first week, my partner and I had been humiliated by a couple of flocks of old gobblers. When we switched our attention to brood flocks, we couldn't find them.

Every time I stopped at an intersection, some guy would stick his head out of his pickup and yell, "I got a nice one yesterday, John. Have you killed yours yet?" I looked forward to the end of exam week at the university when my teaching obligations would cease and I would be free to go after them with *intensity*.

Neither my partner nor I found them in the first four afternoons of exam week. On Thursday I returned home with a very sore back to hear Nell say, "Well, Gary just called and said,

'Bingo!' " I was so tired that the news was a challenge rather than a thrill. I called Gary and he told me the exciting story. He had scattered a flock of gobblers and killed a mature bird on the flush. He could not go back in the morning, but he told me I could find the scatter point without difficulty.

In the morning, for the first time since my last surgery, I had significant pain radiating down my leg. Nevertheless, I put on all my gear in the vain hope it would loosen up. Maybe if I could begin, the adrenaline would kick in and I would be able to hunt. An attempt to walk to my vehicle convinced me the pain was too much. It was Friday, December 15.

I did not think about hunting for the next week. The pain remained and I was sure I faced another surgery. My primary concern was whether I could recover in time to teach in the winter semester, which started on January 8.

I did my best to not allow the pain to ruin Christmas for my family. On the day after Christmas, I made an appointment to see a neurosurgeon. His tests indicated that I had not lost function or nerve responses in my leg, and he suggested I try a spinal shot. Three previous spinal shots had been ineffective, so I had little optimism. I had the shot on Friday, December 29. The next day I felt much better; still, I knew that incapacitating back pain can return at any time. By Tuesday, January 2, I felt so good I looked at the calendar: Saturday the 6th was the last day of the turkey season. I began to wonder if I might be able to hunt again. I took a long walk on Wednesday and felt strong. On Friday I asked my daughter, who was home from college, if she would like to go out with me to search for the flock. We had a great afternoon, found a lot of sign, and even flushed a bird. I decided to try going the next morning—the last day—to a small knoll close to where I had flushed the bird. I felt excited as I put my gear together in the evening. That night the local news indicated we were about to get a huge snowfall that would start the next afternoon. I liked it; I knew the birds would be feeding actively before the storm.

When I woke before the alarm, I looked out to see snow falling heavily. Too much snow, I thought, and turned off the alarm. The first thing Nell said when she woke was, "Is your back all right?" I said that it was, but the snow looked too heavy. Nell said, "I'm sorry." At seven o'clock I got out of bed and noticed that the falling snow seemed very dry and light, and the accumulation was modest. I wondered if a late start might be possible. I turned on the television and heard the excited local newscaster announce that this might be the largest snowfall in decades, with an anticipated twenty-plus inches. My mind began to spin: It would be silly to drive out into the teeth of the storm. There was a good N.F.L. playoff game on television. The pain in my back radiated down my leg. The physician had warned me, *"Do not overdo it."*

I looked out the window and knew I was going. Nell came down the stairs, and I turned to her. "I am thinking about going out in this; would you mind?" Her response was, "I trust your judgment, and would love for you to be able to go." It was almost ten-thirty, but I hurried to the gun room to grab my gear.

It was eleven o'clock when I approached the bridge across Buffalo Creek. Up until this point the road had been clear and the progress had been easy. The farm I intended to hunt was on the other side of the bridge, and I now noticed the road across it was not plowed. I could not have driven much more than the hundred yards or so of unplowed snow that took me to the Leech home. I could not get up the driveway in my non-four-wheel-drive vehicle. It was not starting well. I saw Mr. Leech in the barn and walked over to him. He greeted me pleasantly and explained that the "primary" designation for the road ended one hundred yards from his house. I asked if I could leave the car on the edge of the road, and he said that would be fine.

I felt a bit strange walking down the main road with my Benelli. It was eleven-oh-five when I entered the woods. The snow was falling at a steady rate, but it was so dry that the accumulation was still modest. I guessed there were three inches on the ground. It would be fine for tracking. Would turkeys leave the roost in the face of such a storm? Despite what you often read, it was my guess that they would. My plan was to go up to the knoll where I had planned to be at daylight. It would take me about thirty minutes to get there. I felt cold pain in my right hip as I began the tough climb. It was distracting, but it did not get worse as I climbed. For the first fifteen minutes I did not hit a track of any kind. The grade became steeper, and my confidence began to erode.

It was eleven twenty-five when I got to the knoll. I enjoyed seeing fresh deer tracks as I crested the ridge. A short twenty yards farther on I saw the beautiful triangular tracks—at least four sets of them, and they looked big. Gobblers! Right where I would have been at dawn. Some snow had accumulated in the prints, but I doubted they were more than thirty minutes old. I headed in pursuit, oblivious to the pain. I tried to look out forty or fifty yards in front of the tracks in hope of seeing the birds before they were able to flush. The tracks were so bold that I could easily follow them in my peripheral vision. Soon I came to a place where the birds had scratched in the snow. There was a good bit of fallen snow in the scratching, and I guessed they were still fifteen minutes in front of me. They continued to go down the mountain, and I realized that we were headed for a power line that cut through the hardwoods. As I approached the line, I heard a turkey flush. I raced through the thick cover and saw a bird jump up at a range of about seventy-five yards. I heard other birds go out but did not see them. I arrived at the power line with the sinking realization that I had not only missed an opportunity for a shot but also failed to scatter the flock. I looked at my watch: eleven twenty-eight. It had taken me less than an hour to find the flock.

Now in the middle of the day, with the snow falling hard and poor odds of calling a gobbler, I wondered if it made sense to risk not being able to get back to town in the heavy snowstorm. Despite the odds, I had to try.

I climbed to the small knoll and assessed the blind I had called from several times before. I added some branches to it and cleaned out the interior. By the time I finished my preparations, it was noon. I took my down vest, head net, and calls out of my fanny pack and prepared to wait. I was tired after the excitement and exertion of the past hour, so I ate one of my two emergency candy bars for quick energy. The combination of the warmth of the down vest and the calories of the sugar hit my body, and I began to feel better. The odds were not good, but I began to look forward to the calling.

The woods were extremely quiet. I put my Morgan call to my mouth, adjusting and readjusting it on my lip until it finally felt correct. I usually enjoy hearing the Morgan, but this time I didn't think it sounded good, and I got angry. It just had not been a good year and it seemed unrealistic to hope my luck was going to change. At twelve-fifteen I made another series of calls. If anything, they sounded worse than my first series. It was not going to happen. I focused on the snow and thought about packing it in. I had given it an effort. I had tried. I didn't need a turkey. There had been many great years, and it was silly to stay and risk being unable to make it back to town. These were gobblers and they had been hunted since the end of October. Sitting in the cold blind was terrible for my back. I might not be able to get back to the car, which would cause my family terrible anxiety.

Still I could not convince myself to leave the blind. I did grow impatient, and at twelve twenty-five made another call. It sounded a bit better. I continued to wait, trying to maintain my vigilance despite my lack of hope. My determination to maintain a level of competence made me stay focused, and I avoided unnecessary movement.

When my eyes found him, the recognition was instant. It sounds trite, but he appeared from nowhere. One instant I was scanning a barren ridgetop; the next the full body of a wild turkey gobbler was there. He was stationary, twenty yards away, and his eyes were fixed on me. How he reached his position without my seeing any movement or hearing a sound is one of the great mysteries of his kind. If he had called or made the sounds a walking turkey makes on fallen leaves, the kill would have been childishly easy. He had made what should have been easy exceedingly difficult, as only a gobbler can.

My now-engaged mind said, "Do not move. Be ready for a shot if he moves." A second later he took a cautious step forward and I felt myself look for a tree, in the hope it might screen him from me and give me a chance to bring up my gun. He moved several steps. I had no time. The gun came up. I had a vague, blurred image of him turning quickly when the recoil of the gun hit me. My brain registered a hit. An instant later I saw the bird in the air, and I had a horrible sinking feeling as he disappeared behind the trees.

I stepped out of the blind, and the wrenching reality of a crippled bird overwhelmed me. I walked to the spot where the gobbler had been without any real plan. There were many feathers on the ground—I counted forty—and I tried to assess what had occurred. I saw where some of the shot cut through the snow as it approached him, and where his wings pounded the snow as he flushed. I walked in the direction in which he had flown and saw more feathers that he lost after taking flight. The feathers were from his body, and from their small size I guessed they came from his flanks. I walked back to my blind and sat down to replay the event in the hope of collecting more data. As I put my gun onto my lap, the frustration of the entire year consumed me and, without thinking, I slammed my left hand into the tree, hard. It hurt my wrist, and I was embarrassed by the senseless act. Accepting the loss of a turkey gobbler that was called into sure killing range on the *last day* of the season was not easy.

After several minutes of grim reflection, I got up from the blind and walked to where the bird had been. I was not optimistic, but I would search hard, because I was sure the bird was seriously wounded. From past experience I knew that turkeys will often die in the air and fall to the ground. I also knew that if he were able to walk, the snow would be a tremendous advantage in picking up his track. With these facts in mind, I headed in the direction he had flown.

My plan was to search as carefully as I could for at least five hundred yards, not just in a straight line, but casting from side to side in the general direction of his flight. After twenty minutes I stopped to rest. I had staggered up and down gullies, slipped on ice, tripped over hidden limbs, and generally punished myself. I reflected on my neurosurgeon's words: "Don't try to do too much." I felt my cold, tight face smile at the thought, and in a perverse way I enjoyed my failure to comply with the wise counsel. After half an hour I was four hundred yards from the blind and climbing a steep incline. I knew there was a big open field at the top of the ridge. It was an important place to search. I finally got to the edge of the field and saw nothing. I was soaked with sweat from the climb and fatigue. Frustration and disappointment began to erode my hope. Ideas of "inherent bad luck" and the sense that nothing would turn my terrible year around entered my mind. I tried to maintain my concentration.

The pervasive fatigue brought darker thoughts to my mind: "You are not lucky enough to find this bird. It could happen to Gary, but it will not happen to you." I also reflected with some self-pity on my surgeries. I made a big swing to the south before turning back toward the blind, covering a different swath of ground. At the forty-minute mark, I cut turkey tracks, but they had too much snow in them to be my bird. I felt no temptation to follow them. I was not hunting turkeys now, but a specific bird. Back at the blind, I decided to make my last search to the north of the path I thought the bird had taken. The area seemed unlikely. The first hundred yards were in open hardwoods, and then I entered a rather dense thicket of cedars. The reduced visibility did not help my spirits. I realized I was well into the second hour of my search and I struggled to maintain my concentration.

At first, I thought it was a strange growth of mushrooms peeking out of the snow at the base of the dark "stump." My attention was attracted. At fifteen yards the "mushrooms" begin to look like feathers. At ten yards there was no question that they were feathers—turkey tail feathers! I rushed awkwardly to the feature and dropped to my knees next to the dead turkey. I felt an incredible surge of adrenaline and, with no concern for who might hear me, thrust my arms into the air and screamed, "Yes!"

As I picked up the bird, I saw that the shot had raked his underbelly and legs. He no doubt died of internal hemorrhaging while in the air. The spot where he hit the snow indicated he had not landed but crashed to the ground after dying in the air. I know he was pumping his wings with all the power his great courage could generate when his systems shut down. He fell more than two hundred yards from where he had flushed.

The fact that I had found the turkey gave me pride. I understood the good fortune involved, but it was my persistence that brought a warmth and calmness. It would have been easy to give up my search after the first hour. I arrogantly reflected that only a few hunters would have persevered. I am proud to have earned their company. The walk back to the car with the sixteen-pound bird was joyful. My entire body was sore, and there was a sharp pain in my hip, but the victory overcame the discomfort.

Nell and my two daughters celebrated the turkey. In fact, I reported to them on my car phone shortly after I started the adventure of driving back into the face of the blizzard. My excuse for calling was to see if any check-in stations were still open in the storm, but I really wanted to let them know I had killed the gobbler. It was fun to hear their excitement at the news.

I passed two four-wheel-drive vehicles in a ditch. When I reached the house I was so stiff I laughed at myself as I struggled out of the car, but I was incredibly happy. It was not just the wonderful bird and the great day etched in my mind; it was so much more, a wonderful sense of satisfaction and accomplishment. As is true of many turkey hunts, I learned about myself. I will enjoy my own company more as a function of the experience. No one was there to see it, and only I know that the story is impeccably honest, but the experience will become part of me and give me confidence, pride, and a strength that is hard to acquire in most domains of contemporary human endeavor.